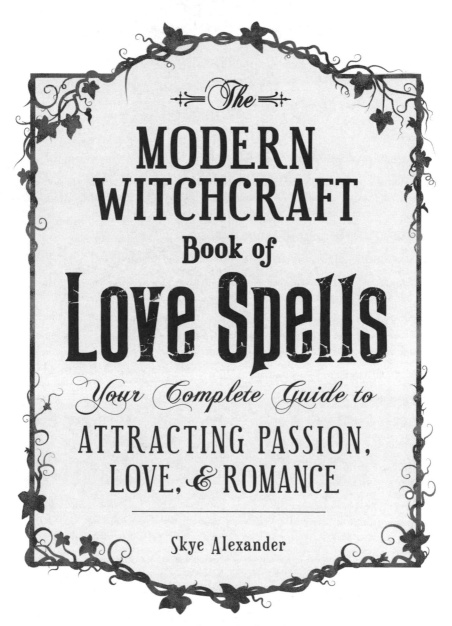

The
MODERN WITCHCRAFT
Book of
Love Spells

Your Complete Guide to

ATTRACTING PASSION, LOVE, & ROMANCE

Skye Alexander

Adams Media

New York London Toronto Sydney New Delhi

To my beloved Ron, your magick lives on. Love never dies.

Adams Media

An Imprint of Simon & Schuster, Inc.

100 Technology Center Drive

Stoughton, MA 02072

First Adams Media hardcover edition JULY 2017

ADAMS MEDIA and colophon are trademarks of Simon and Schuster.

For information about special discounts for bulk purchases, please contact Simon & Schuster Special Sales at 1-866-506-1949 or business@simonandschuster.com.

The Simon & Schuster Speakers Bureau can bring authors to your live event. For more information or to book an event contact the Simon & Schuster Speakers Bureau at 1-866-248-3049 or visit our website at www.simonspeakers.com.

Interior design by Colleen Cunningham

Manufactured in China

10 9 8 7

Library of Congress Cataloging-in-Publication Data has been applied for.

ISBN 978-1-5072-0363-7
ISBN 978-1-5072-0364-4 (ebook)

Acknowledgments

Once again, I am indebted to my astute and supportive editors Rebecca Tarr Thomas and Peter Archer, and to the rest of the Adams Media staff for making this book a reality. Thanks, too, to Stephanie Hannus for her beautiful cover design. Finally, I wish to thank my many readers worldwide who have encouraged me throughout the development of this book—without you none of this would have happened.

CONTENTS

Chapter 3: SPELLCASTING WITH CRYSTALS AND GEMSTONES 49

Chapter 4: PLANT MAGICK 69

Chapter 5: TALISMANS AND AMULETS 85

Chapter 6: VISUAL SPELLS 101

Chapter 7: LOVE POTIONS AND LOTIONS 119

Chapter 8: EDIBLE SPELLS 135

Chapter 9: SPELLS TO HONOR THE SEASONS AND SPECIAL DAYS 151

Chapter 10: SPELLS AND RITUALS TO DO WITH A PARTNER 167

Chapter 11: MISCELLANEOUS SPELLS 183

Chapter 12: WHAT'S THE NEXT STEP? 199

Index 204

INTRODUCTION

As Shakespeare wrote in his play *A Midsummer Night's Dream*, "The course of true love never did run smooth." That's why witches cast more love spells than any other kind. You may already have done love spells yourself; you just didn't realize it. Hanging mistletoe above a doorway, for example, is a favorite pagan love spell. Toasting a bride and groom's happiness has magickal roots, and dancing around a Maypole is an age-old fertility ritual.

Since ancient times, people have done spells to attract a new lover, increase a partner's ardor, smooth the bumps in a relationship, or ward off an unwanted suitor. We still do—perhaps you picked up this book for one of these reasons.

HOW DO SPELLS WORK?

In his book *Modern Magick*, Donald Michael Kraig explains, "Magick is not something you do! Magick is something you are." You don't put it on and take it off when the mood strikes you. Magick is a way of viewing the world, of understanding your connection with everything in the universe, and believing in the innate power that resides within you. When witches cast spells or perform magick rituals, what we're really doing is expressing outwardly what we are inside.

When you do magick, you align yourself with the energetic forces operating on earth and beyond. You serve as a conduit for these energies and direct them to produce results in the manifest world. Both the Law of Attraction and quantum physics tell us that our thoughts affect our reality, so the most important factor in magick is your mind.

Many witches find candles, crystals, magick wands, and other tools helpful in spellcraft because they focus your attention and shift your thinking from mundane to magickal. The spells in this book show you how to use special objects and techniques to hone your own creative powers.

HOW TO USE THIS BOOK

Perhaps you're already a practicing witch and want some new love spells to add to your repertoire. Or, you may be a newbie just starting out on this path. Either way, this book is for you. Chapter 1 covers the basics of spellworking in a user-friendly manner. I encourage beginners to become familiar with this information—and to explore other sources for more about what I touch upon here.

The rest of the book is an open grimoire of 150 love spells. Here you'll find potions and lotions, talismans and amulets, affirmations and incantations, and a lot more. If you're a novice, I suggest trying these spells as given until you tone your magickal muscles and feel confident in your ability. Later on, I urge you to design your own spells and practice them with your partner to enhance your love and enrich your lives. You may even want to share them with other like-minded people. Whatever you deem right for you *is*. Blessed be.

Chapter 1

THE ART OF CRAFTING AND CASTING LOVE SPELLS

If you're like many people, you first encountered love spells in fairy tales. As a child, you saw Cinderella's Fairy Godmother transform a pumpkin into a jeweled coach drawn by a team of prancing horses so the heroine could attend Prince Charming's ball. You heard a story about a princess who kissed a frog and turned him into a handsome prince. Another tale told of a prince whose kiss removed an evil spell, reviving Sleeping Beauty from a deathlike trance. Then you grew up and put away your belief in magick.

Now, however, you may be wondering if magick really does exist and, if so, can it help you? That's why you picked up this book, right? Perhaps you've got your eye on someone, but he or she doesn't seem to notice you exist. Or maybe a romantic relationship has lost its sparkle and you want to rekindle the flame. You've tried all the usual stuff, yet nothing appears to be working. Could a love spell give you the edge you need?

Absolutely. Magick really does work—it happens all the time. Furthermore, you already have magickal ability—you were born with it, just like everyone else. As with all natural abilities, it needs to be developed so you can craft and cast spells effectively to consciously create the circumstances you desire. That's what this book and the other books in my Modern Witchcraft series are designed to help you do.

GETTING STARTED

Magick is all about working with energy. Energy, as you know, is the raw material that makes up our universe—everything is composed of energy. When you do magick, you activate energy and shape it with your willpower to produce results in the manifest world. That may sound mysterious, but it's not really. Quantum physics has demonstrated that when you focus your attention on something, your energy influences the behavior of the molecules you're watching. You quite literally change whatever you observe. That's magick.

Why Add the K?

Witches, wizards, shamans, and others who work with the magickal forces of the universe sometimes add the letter *k* to the word *magic* to distinguish it from stage illusion, card tricks, and the like. Aleister Crowley, one of the most notorious magicians of the twentieth century, is often credited with implementing this change.

What Spells Are and Aren't

Simply put, a spell is something you do with clarity, intent, and awareness to generate a result. A spell usually includes a series of thoughts and symbolic actions performed in the physical world to initiate change on a higher level. Once a change takes place at that higher level, it filters down and manifests here on earth. You alter a situation by introducing new energy or rearranging the energy that's already present.

When doing a spell, you act as the agent of change. You draw upon your own resources to gather and direct energy. You may request assistance from a higher power to accomplish your objective, if you wish. Or, you may bring in the energies of various substances, such as plants and gemstones, to augment your own powers. Ultimately, however, you're the writer, director, and producer of this drama.

A spell is *not* a religious act, though some people choose to work with goddesses, gods, or other deities. Properly done, spells aren't dangerous; they're not uncommon, difficult, or weird. They're a natural, intentional, and time-honored method for directing the course of your life, instead of passively accepting whatever comes your way.

The Importance of Intention

Before you even begin a magick spell, you must have a goal, often called an intention. This is the outcome you wish to accomplish, and you must be absolutely clear about your intention, otherwise you won't achieve the results you desire. Think of it this way: When you set out on a trip, you need to know your destination if you expect to get there. The same holds true in spellwork.

What's your reason for doing a love spell? Are you trying to attract a new romantic partner? Hoping to increase the passion in an existing relationship? Do you want to end an unfulfilling partnership on good terms? The more specific you can be, the greater your chances of success.

> *"Relationships are the Holy Spirit's laboratories in which He brings together people who have the maximal opportunity for mutual growth. He appraises who can learn most from whom at any given time, and then assigns them to each other."*
> —MARIANNE WILLIAMSON, *A RETURN TO LOVE*

Keep in mind that a love spell's primary purpose isn't to force someone to fall in love with you or do your bidding (we'll talk more about this soon). Its purpose is to work with your own energy, the other person's energy, and that which is inherent in the universe to create a relationship that's in the best interests of all concerned.

Focusing Your Attention

Once you've set your intention, you need to focus your attention toward achieving that goal. Every athlete knows you must keep your attention keenly focused on the game if you want to play well. "Keep your eye on the ball" is the mantra all baseball players, golfers, and tennis stars learn from day one. The same holds true when you're doing magick. Keep your attention on your objective. The more energy you can marshal and direct toward that objective, the more successful you'll be.

> *"If you focus upon whatever you want, you will attract whatever you want. If you focus upon the lack of whatever you want, you will attract more of the lack."*
> —ESTHER AND JERRY HICKS, *THE LAW OF ATTRACTION*

One of the best ways I know to hone your attention is to meditate. Daily meditation—even if it's only for ten minutes at a time—helps clear the static from your mind, calm your emotions, and connect you with higher levels of awareness. Basketball stars Michael Jordan and Kobe Bryant, for example, are only a couple of the many noted athletes who credit meditation as an aid to their success. You may also consider doing yoga, chanting, martial arts, or various other practices designed to improve attention.

Magick rituals often involve carefully choreographed steps designed to keep the magician on track. Spellworkers also use a number of tools to help them focus their minds and shift from a mundane to a magickal level of consciousness. These include candles, crystals, scents, images, incantations, music, and more. Witches work with four principal tools:

- The wand, used to direct energy
- The chalice, used for holding libations
- The athame (ritual dagger), used symbolically to cut ties and obstacles
- The pentagram, used for protection

Many of the spells in this book incorporate these tools and others, as you'll soon see. Remember, however, that the tools aren't the source of magick—you are. Your mind, your energy, your willpower create the magick; tools and rituals simply sharpen your attention and help you be more effective.

Magi

The word *magician* comes from the Latin word *magi* (the plural of *magus*), which can be translated as "wise men or women." The best-known magi are the Three Wise Men referred to in the Bible, who came from the East to offer gifts to the baby Jesus. Magi can be healers, shamans, priests or priestesses, astrologers, dowsers, seers—anyone who has learned to access the cosmic web of energy and information that animates the universe, and to direct it for his or her purposes.

AFFIRMATIONS AND INCANTATIONS

The earliest spells were probably verbal ones. At a time when few people could read and write, verbal spells were understandably popular. Early grimoires (witches' spell books and journals) included eloquent calls to the gods and goddesses—as well as other nonphysical entities—for magickal purposes.

When you utter a spell aloud, you create a resonance that begins the process of manifestation. Sounds produce vibrations that echo through the cosmic web that connects everything in our universe.

These vibrations stimulate effects in the visible world. Words also act as verbal symbols to convey your intentions. One of the best-known magick words is *abracadabra*, which some scholars assert derives from the Aramaic *avra kehdabra* (also *avarah k'davarah*, etc.), meaning "I will create as I speak."

The Power of Prayer

Prayer can play a key role in magick work. According to Larry Dossey, MD, author of *Healing Words* and *Prayer Is Good Medicine*, in cases of intercessory prayer (praying for someone else at a distance), the consciousness of the person who is doing the praying actually influences the body of the person being prayed for.

Creating Affirmations and Incantations

Words have the power to influence outcomes. Whether you speak your intentions aloud or write them down on paper, putting your goals into words helps focus your mind and energize your spells. The magick of words has a long, time-honored tradition. The Gospel of John in the Bible, for example, links "the Word" with the power of creation. Buddhists chant mantras, such as *Om Mani Padme Hum*, to invoke blessings from deities. The ancient alpha/numeric system known as gematria equates each letter with a number, and each number has a specific resonance; therefore, you can understand the hidden meaning of a word or phrase if you know its numeric value. In the 1980s, Japanese author and researcher Masaru Emoto asserted that words, either written or spoken, could alter the molecular structure of water.

Many magick spells and rituals include special words, phrases, statements, poems, chants, or prayers. As you might expect, some ways of verbalizing your intentions are more effective than others.

Affirmations are positive statements you design to produce a result—for example, "I now have a mutually joyful and fulfilling primary partnership." When writing an affirmation:

- Keep it short.
- Be clear and precise.
- Only include images and situations you desire.
- Always use the present tense.

Incantations differ from affirmations in that they are usually written as rhymes—for example, "I love you and you love me / And we shall always joyful be." The catchy phrasing makes the incantation easy to remember. You don't have to be a Wordsworth or Dickinson to create an effective incantation; the important thing is to follow the same rules when writing an incantation as when writing an affirmation. You can add an affirmation or incantation to any spell, or just use the statement as a spell in itself. Throughout this book you'll find spells that use affirmations and incantations—I encourage you to design your own and incorporate them into your magick work.

A PICTURE'S WORTH A THOUSAND WORDS

As powerful as affirmations and incantations are, pictures are even more potent in spellworking. Your subconscious responds better to images than words. Images speak directly to your inner self. Symbols and pictures bypass the analytical, orderly left brain and communicate with the creative, intuitive right brain—that's why they're so useful in magick work.

Your mind forms pictures all the time. Notice what happens when you read the word *camel*. Immediately, an image of a large humped creature springs into your mind; from there you may spin off all sorts of pictures, such as an Arab riding across a desert with pyramids in the background. In spellcasting the goal is to design pictures that hold meaning for you and that epitomize your objective. What you see is what you'll get.

Using Colors in Spells

One of the most common and important visuals you'll use in your spellwork is color. Colors influence us in countless ways, whether or not we realize it, and we make symbolic associations with colors. For example, we link red with passion and pink with affection. Therefore, you'll use pink and red in many love spells. Other colors, too, hold meanings you can tap to add octane to your spells, as you'll learn in Chapter 6.

Symbols

Symbols are more than a convenient form of shorthand; they're visual metaphors. Symbols encapsulate the essence of whatever they represent. A good logo, for instance, is a symbol that reveals important information about a company: Rolex's crown bespeaks royalty; Nike's signature "check mark" connotes speed. The heart, of course, signifies love, and you'll use hearts often in love spells. Roses and diamonds also have romantic associations. You may have some unique, personal symbols as well that hold meaning for you alone.

Numbers are among the most common symbols in our lives. They're not only tools for keeping score; they also possess secret meanings that make them valuable in working magick. The number two, for instance, plays a part in a lot of love spells. We even use the term *couple* to refer to two things and to people joined in a romantic relationship. Each number has distinct meanings you can tap in your spellwork, which we'll discuss in Chapter 6.

Take some time to consider what various symbols mean to you and which ones hold significance. Any image you relate to in a deep way, that triggers your emotions and imagination, can be useful in spellwork. Chapter 6 contains all sorts of spells that use symbols, colors, numbers, and pictures.

A TIME FOR MAGICK

What's the best time to do a spell? That depends on your objective. In magickal practice *when* you do spells and rituals can be as important as *how* you do them. For best results, you'll want to consider not only factors here on earth but also those operating in the heavens.

"To every thing there is a season, and a time to every purpose under the heaven."

—Ecclesiastes 3:1, King James Bible

Lunar Cycles

Witches pay attention to the moon when doing magick work, in part because the moon represents the Goddess and the feminine principle in the universe. Additionally, the moon influences our emotions, creativity, fertility, and cycles in our world. Of course, we also link the moon with romance, mystery, and magick. When doing love spells, consider four phases of the moon:

- The new moon nurtures beginnings, so if your intention is to start a new relationship, cast a spell on the new moon.

- The waxing moon supports growth; therefore spells to increase love, romance, affection, passion, or happiness can benefit from the waxing moon's energy.
- The full moon represents fulfillment and culmination; it's a good time to do spells to celebrate your love or bring about a conclusion, such as a marriage.
- The waning moon encourages decrease; do spells to end a relationship during this phase.

Also note the astrological sign in which the moon is positioned at the time. Taurus and Libra are ruled by Venus, the planet astrologers connect with love and relationships. In most cases you'll want to perform love spells when the moon is in one of these signs. However, if your objective is to kick up your relationship a notch or improve your sex life, you could cast a spell when the moon is in Aries. To stabilize a relationship or end one, do the spell when the moon is in Capricorn.

The Days of the Week

The heavenly bodies not only govern the signs of the zodiac; they also preside over the days of the week:

- Monday: Moon
- Tuesday: Mars
- Wednesday: Mercury
- Thursday: Jupiter
- Friday: Venus
- Saturday: Saturn
- Sunday: Sun

You can boost the power of your spell by performing it on a day that resonates with favorable celestial energies. Venus, the planet of love and relationships, is in charge on Friday; therefore most love spells can be done effectively on Fridays. Spells to spark passion are best performed on Tuesday; those to enhance communication on Wednesday; and those for endings or banishing on Saturday.

If you know astrology, you may also want to consider the impact of the sun's movement through the signs, planetary aspects and transits, retrograde periods, and planetary hours. In Chapter 9 we'll talk about the advantages of spellworking on holidays and other special dates.

CASTING A CIRCLE

Witches and other magickal workers usually cast a protective circle around the space where they perform spells and rituals. A magick circle provides an energetic barrier that keeps unwanted energies out and holds desired energies in until you're ready to release them. Your circle may be invisible or physical, temporary or permanent, indoors or out, but it will always contain a powerful psychic, spiritual component. When you're inside a circle, you are "between the worlds," present in the physical and the spirit realms simultaneously—and you'll be able to feel the energetic differences within the circle and outside.

Creating an Altar

Many witches set up altars for magickal purposes. An altar serves as a "workbench" where you cast spells, perform rites and rituals, commune with deities and spirits, and meditate. You go there temporarily to leave the ordinary, everyday world behind and enter sacred space. An altar may also house your magick tools, clothing, ingredients for spells, images of goddesses and gods—anything you include in spells and rituals. Depending on your space and living situation, you may choose to create a permanent altar in the place where you do magick, or a temporary one you can set up and dismantle as necessary.

Preparing Your Magick Space

Before you cast the circle, however, cleanse the area in which you plan to do your spell or ritual. Sweep away dirt and old energies with a broom—that's the real reason witches use brooms, not to fly through the sky. Remove any objects that don't pertain to your purpose. Smudge the area by burning sage or incense. Doing this not only chases away bad vibes; it also helps you start getting in the mood to work magick.

Grounding and Centering

You may have heard the term *grounding and centering*. This step connects you with the earth and yourself before you engage in magick work. However, you can ground and center in your daily life too.

Some people *ground* by imagining themselves growing "roots" that sink deep into the earth, roots that provide stability and draw up energy the way a tree's roots draw nourishment. Other people hold a smoky quartz crystal, lie on the ground, do yoga, or drum. You may want to take a ritual bath, anoint yourself with aromatic oils, or dress in special clothing—do whatever makes you feel secure and connected to Mother Earth.

Centering can take any form that enables you to feel balanced and peaceful. The point is to harmonize your emotions, calm your mind, let go of everyday concerns, and connect with your inner self. Meditate, chant, pray, play music—whatever lets you shift your thinking from mundane to magickal.

Basic Circle-Casting Techniques

The ritual of casting a circle can be as simple or complex as you want it to be. The quickest and easiest is to close your eyes, relax, and envision a sphere of pure white light surrounding you and the space where you will be working. In your mind's eye fill the space with love, protection, peace, and power. Another popular technique is performed with a magick wand or athame (a witch's magickal dagger), but if you don't have one of these tools you can just use your finger.

1. Stand in the center of the space that will be enclosed by your circle and face east.
2. With your arm outstretched, point your wand, athame, or finger toward the spot where you'll begin casting the circle.
3. Turn slowly in a clockwise direction, using your wand, athame, or finger to draw a circle as you envision it forming around you. Make sure you will be within the circle when you're finished. You may even see a whitish mist or glowing light flowing out from the tip of your tool and encircling you.
4. When you've completed a 360-degree circuit, drop your arm to stop the flow of energy.
5. Imagine the circle expanding, stretching above you and beneath you to form a sphere.

Now you're ready to enact your spell or ritual.

When you've finished your spell or ritual, reverse your steps to remove the protective barrier you erected and release your magick into the world: Start in the east again and move in a counterclockwise direction. Envision the energy you previously projected outward now being sucked back into your wand, athame, or finger as you open the circle.

This book contains a few more methods for casting circles, including one in Chapter 10 that you can do with a partner. You'll also find a number of circle-casting practices described in my other books in the Modern Witchcraft series, as well as in many other books. Some involve petitioning deities, angels, and spirits to assist you. Others draw upon the four elements: fire, earth, water, and air. You can even build a permanent circle using stone or other materials if you have a place for it; Stonehenge is perhaps the best known of all magickal stone circles.

"Magick is the spice of life, and it turns a relationship into a feast of sensual pleasures."
—SIRONA KNIGHT, *LOVE, SEX, AND MAGICK*

ETHICAL SPELLCASTING

Love makes the world go round, as the saying goes, and more magick spells are cast for matters of the heart than for any other purpose. Because emotion is one of the key ingredients in magick, it's logical that love spells would be among the most powerful of all. Strong feelings, however, can sometimes cause confusion or throw you off balance. Therefore love spells tend to be the trickiest of all to perform, and they are the most likely to tempt magicians to stray to the dark side. That's not to say spellcasters hex their partners or wish anything evil to happen. But the heart isn't rational and emotions can interfere with good judgment. When you want someone really badly, it can be hard to refrain from using magick to manipulate that person.

What makes a spell manipulative? The main criterion is whether it violates another person's free will. You don't have to actively harm someone to misuse magick. You're treading on shaky ground any time you force or coerce a person through magickal means to do something he or she wouldn't ordinarily do of his or her own volition. Whenever your desire to get what you want overshadows your respect for another person's rights, you're leaning in the wrong direction.

Consider the possible consequences—are you willing to accept what happens? Would you advise your best friend to do it? How would you react if someone did it to you? Trust your feelings—if you don't feel right about it, don't do it.

Not everyone will agree with me on these definitions, but in my opinion:

- Black magick means anything done to harm someone else.
- White magick is done to obtain higher knowledge, evolve spiritually, or strengthen your connection with the Source.
- Gray magick includes everything else.

The Best Way to Do Love Spells

Let's say you're interested in a certain individual and want to entice that person into a romantic relationship. Your intention and the way you word a spell can make a big difference in the quality of the outcome. Instead of stating, "Josh and I are now lovers," you could word your affirmation in a more positive way, such as: "Josh and I now enjoy the best possible relationship we can have together." Then, if it's best for the two of you to be lovers, that's what will happen. If, on the other hand, another type of relationship would better serve you and Josh, you'll put yourself in a position to experience what's right for both of you. The best love spells respect all persons involved, while also trusting the universe and your inner knowing to guide you.

Doing Spells with a Partner

When it comes to doing magick, two hearts can be better than one—provided you are in agreement. The blend of yin and yang energies forms a strong, balanced creative force. Doing a spell with a partner to increase the love between you can be a powerful and beautiful experience. Many couples do magick together to conceive a child, to attract prosperity, or for other joint purposes.

Before you begin, discuss your intentions and your feelings about the spell you plan to do. Each of you should have input in designing and casting the spell. Unless one person is significantly more skilled than the other, try to make your roles in the ritual equal so that neither partner dominates. Remember, the outcome will affect both of you.

Chapter 10 is devoted to spells and rituals designed for you to enact with your beloved. Many of the spells in the rest of this book can be shared with a partner—or even an extended network of loved ones and magick workers. Feel free to adapt them to suit your needs.

Magick isn't a rigid dogma; it's an ever-evolving, co-creative experience that benefits from the input of everyone who embraces it. Your wisdom, your imagination, and your power enhance everyone else's. Together we grow and prosper. Blessed be.

Chapter 2

CANDLE SPELLS

The term *candle* comes from *candere*, a Latin word meaning "to shine" or "to make bright." Candles brighten many of our secular and religious celebrations, including Christmas and Hanukkah (a.k.a. Chanukah). In our everyday lives we light candles when we want to create an elegant, serene, or sensual mood—what would a romantic dinner be without candlelight?

Candles are the most common and versatile tool you're likely to use in your magick work, and they play a role in a lot of rituals and spells. The concept of illumination carries both a practical meaning—visible light that enables you to see to conduct your daily tasks—and an esoteric one—an inspiration or awakening that expands your understanding. In spellwork the flame represents clarity, passion, activity, energy, and purification.

Candle History

According to Patricia Telesco, in her book *Exploring Candle Magick*, "Something resembling modern candles started to appear around the 1200s. This is when we see the first dipped tapers made from tallow and beeswax. . . . Candle-molding techniques followed in the 1400s, making candles more accessible to the general public. . . . In the late 1500s, the Catholic church started using red candles at mass because it seemed to improve the impact of sermons on those in attendance."

USING CANDLES IN SPELLWORK

Candles symbolize the fire element and Spirit, the energizing force that activates spells and rituals. When you're casting a spell, candles provide a focal point for your attention—they help still your mind so you can concentrate on your objective. Their soft, flickering light also creates a peaceful ambiance that shifts you out of your ordinary existence and into a magickal realm.

Birthday Candle Magick

You've probably already done a simple and popular candle spell: making a wish and then blowing out candles on a birthday cake. As astrologers know, cosmic energies are generally favorable on your birthday, so this is an ideal time to do magick.

Candles can enhance just about any spell. Many magick workers set candles on their altars to honor the divine forces present in our lives. White, red, and gold candles symbolize masculine/yang/god; black, blue, and silver candles represent feminine/yin/goddess energies. Some formal rituals involve carefully placing candles in specific spots and moving them according to prescribed patterns over a period. Some of the spells in this book use this technique as well.

Here are other ideas for using candles in your magickal workings:

- Cast a circle with candles. Position them around the space where you plan to perform a magick spell or ritual. Then light them in a clockwise manner, beginning at the easternmost point. Extinguish them in a counterclockwise manner.
- When performing a spell or ritual, mark the four directions with candles of corresponding colors. Place a yellow candle in the east, a red one in the south, a blue one in the west, and a green one in the north.

- You may choose to "dress" your candles by rubbing a little essential oil on them (but not on the wicks). This adds another sensory dimension: the power of scent.
- If you like, engrave words, symbols, or sigils into the wax. As the candle burns, your intentions will be released into the universe.

"There are two ways of spreading light: to be the candle or the mirror that reflects it."
—EDITH WHARTON, "VESALIUS IN ZANTE"

As you evolve as a spellcaster, you'll probably want to stock up on candles in various colors, sizes, and shapes. Consider keeping a stash of the following types on hand so you're ready to cast a spell whenever the need or desire arises:

- Tapers are good all-around tools for many spells and add ambiance in both magickal and mundane settings.
- Pillars, which burn for hours, are ideal for spells that take place over a period of days.
- Mini candles and tea lights are efficient choices for short spells.
- Votives, too, can be used for short spells as well as for circle-casting. If you like to work outside you may want to stock up on these candles—their protective glass containers shield them from the wind and can prevent them from blowing out.
- Figure candles represent people in your spells.
- Floating candles add a romantic element in a ritual bath.

Some witches enjoy making their own candles, blending the wax with herbs or flowers, essential oils, and dyes. You can form candle wax into shapes, such as hearts or stars, to represent your objectives. In this chapter you'll find spells that use candles in various ways to produce magickal results.

CANDLE MEDITATION

You can do this meditation anytime to calm and center your mind. Use it to help you focus on an intention, to gain advice in connection with a relationship issue, or as a preliminary to another spell or ritual.

Tools and Ingredients

A white candle in a candleholder

Matches or a lighter

A comfortable chair or meditation cushion

1. Set the candle on your altar, or another place where it can burn safely, and light it.
2. Sit in a comfortable place and position—it's hard to meditate when you feel cramped. Breathe slowly and deeply; relax.
3. Gaze at the candle's flame and let your mind grow calm. Ask for guidance, such as "How can I improve my relationship with [name]?" or "How can I attract a romantic partner who's right for me?"
4. Allow images to emerge in your mind's eye. Don't try to force anything, just observe. Notice any emotions, insights, or impressions that arise.
5. Continue meditating for as long as you like. When you're ready, return to your ordinary consciousness, extinguish the candle, and express thanks for the guidance you've received.

SINGLE CANDLE SPELL TO ATTRACT A NEW LOVER

In this spell, the candle's flame acts as a beacon, shining light into the darkness to guide your lover to you. Begin this spell during the waxing moon, at least three days before the full moon, preferably when the moon is in Taurus or Libra.

Tools and Ingredients

A pink or red candle (your choice) in a candleholder

Matches or a lighter

A piece of silk cloth

1. Place your candle in an east-facing window. East, where the sun rises, is the direction of new beginnings.
2. After dark, light the candle and let it burn for at least ten minutes. Say aloud the following incantation or one you compose yourself.

> *"Magick candle burning bright*
> *Shine your light into the night*
> *And bring to me a love that's right."*

3. Snuff out the candle.
4. Repeat each night until the full moon or until your true love shows up.
5. If you don't meet your lover by the time of the full moon, wrap what's left of the candle in silk and store it until after the new moon; you can begin the spell again at that time. If you do meet your lover before the full moon, give thanks and then wrap what's left of the candle in silk and bury it outside near a tree or body of water.

SEALED WITH A KISS

In days of old, people used wax to seal letters. This spell harkens back to that lovely tradition. It also taps the visual magick of Norse runes to express your intention.

Tools and Ingredients

A pink or red candle in a holder

Matches or a lighter

A piece of pretty paper and an envelope (if you're craft-inclined, you can make your own paper)

A pen that writes red ink

A nail, athame, or other pointed tool

1. Set the candle on a table or desk, or wherever you will be working, and light it.

2. On the paper, write a love letter to your partner or the person you wish to attract.

3. When you've finished, fold the sheet of paper and slip it into the envelope. Hold the candle slightly tilted and drip some of the melted wax onto the flap of the envelope to seal it.

4. After the wax has cooled somewhat but is still soft, inscribe the rune Gebo (a.k.a. Gifu) in the wax with your pointed tool. This rune is a symbol for love; it looks like an X.

5. You may mail the letter to your beloved or lay it on your bedside table. If you know feng shui, you can place it in your Relationship Gua.

"Each of us is born with a box of matches inside us but we can't strike them all by ourselves; . . . we need oxygen and a candle to help."

—Laura Esquivel, *Like Water for Chocolate*

SCENT-SATIONAL CANDLE SPELL

For thousands of years people have used scent to encourage romantic feelings. The ancient Egyptians, for instance, raised aromatic seduction to an art form. Although different people respond to fragrances differently, witches usually associate certain essential oils with love and passion. See Chapter 4 for a table of sensual scents.

Tools and Ingredients

A red candle

A ballpoint pen, nail file, athame, or other pointed tool

Essential oil of rose, ylang-ylang, jasmine, patchouli, musk, or other oil
  you prefer

A candleholder

Matches or a lighter

1. Carve the rune Gebo (a.k.a. Gifu) on the candle with your pointed tool. This rune is a symbol for love; it looks like an X.

2. Pour a little essential oil in your palm and anoint the candle with it.

3. Fit the candle in the holder and light the candle. As it burns, enjoy the rich scent while you hold loving thoughts in your mind. If you like, read a love poem, recite an incantation, or play out a visualization that depicts your intention.

4. When your attention starts to wander, extinguish the candle. Repeat the spell whenever you wish.

REKINDLE THE SPARK IN YOUR RELATIONSHIP

Has the "spark" gone out of your relationship? This spell can help your love shine bright again. Perform the spell alone or with your partner during the waxing moon.

Tools and Ingredients

A short red pillar candle or votive

A flameproof bowl

Matches or a lighter

Clippings of your hair

Clippings of your lover's hair

1. Set the candle in the bowl and place it somewhere you can burn the candle safely (such as a fireplace or barbecue grill); light the candle.

2. Sprinkle the clippings of your hair and your lover's in the flame—be careful not to burn yourself! Say this incantation (or one you compose) aloud:

> *"Magick candle*
> *Burning bright*
> *Spark our love*
> *This very night."*

3. Gaze into the flame for a few minutes, as you sense your love grow stronger. Feel the light of love expanding outward from your heart into the universe.

4. When you're ready, extinguish the candle. End the spell by saying, "This is done in harmony with Divine Will, our own true wills, and with good to all."

MAKE A MAGICK HEART CANDLE

Use your creative talents to attract a lover with this spell. By fashioning this heart-shaped candle, you send a magickal message that you are open to receiving love and you shine a light for a lover to find you. Perform this spell a day or two after the new moon.

Tools and Ingredients

¼ pound wax (paraffin, soy, beeswax, or old candles repurposed); makes about 4–5 ounces melted wax

Newspaper or butcher paper

A knife

A large pot

A 2-cup heat-resistant glass measuring cup (Note: It can be hard to remove the wax from the glass cup, so you may want to purchase one specifically for this purpose.)

Red candle dye (not food coloring)

A candle wick

Optional: essential oil of rose, ylang-ylang, jasmine, patchouli, or musk

Optional: dried red or pink rose petals or other flower petals that suit your intention (see Chapter 4)

1. Place the wax on the paper and slice it into smallish pieces; this will allow it to melt quicker.

2. Put enough water in the pot so that it will cover the measuring cup about halfway.

3. Put the wax in the measuring cup and hang the cup on the edge of the pot so that it is halfway immersed in the water. Heat the water to boiling.

4. Stir the wax, tending it carefully as it melts. Stir using a clockwise motion while you send loving thoughts into the wax.

5. Put a few drops of red coloring into the melted wax and stir.

6. If you've chosen to add scent, put a few drops of essential oil into the melted wax and stir.

7. If you've opted to include flower petals, allow the wax to cool partly but not harden. While the wax is still soft, add the flower petals.

8. While the wax is still warm and pliable, shape it with your fingers to form a pretty pink heart. Position the wick in the center of the wax as you work, molding the heart around the wick. Trim the wick to a manageable length.

9. When the wax has completely cooled and hardened, place the heart (on a heat-resistant plate, stand, or ashtray) in your bedroom. Burn the heart candle for a few minutes each night to attract your perfect mate.

SPELL TO REMOVE NEGATIVE ENERGY

In all but the most enlightened relationships, arguments happen. After a disagreement, or other unpleasant experience, perform this spell to burn away bad vibes and cleanse your environment so that old energies won't interfere with your happiness in the future.

Tools and Ingredients
A black candle in a holder
Matches or a lighter

1. Place the candle in a safe spot, such as a fireplace, where it can burn down completely.

2. Light the candle and imagine the purifying power of fire burning up the negativity as you watch the flame, leaving behind only peaceful, positive energy.

SPELL TO SOFTEN YOUR HEART

If past hurts have caused you to build a protective wall around your heart or you're holding a grudge against your partner, this spell helps melt the resistance that's interfering with your happiness. It also sweetens your feelings. You can perform this spell alone or with your partner. Choose candles in colors you and your partner like, or that relate to your astrological signs.

Tools and Ingredients

A candle (in a candleholder) to symbolize you

A candle (in a candleholder) to symbolize your partner

Matches or a lighter

1 teaspoon warm honey

1. Place the candles on your altar and light them.

2. Put a dab of the soft, warm honey on each candle.

3. Dab a little honey on your chest, near your heart. Put another dab on your tongue. Envision the honey sweetening your love, dissolving all obstacles and hard feelings between you. Imagine your heart opening to your beloved.

4. If you and your partner are doing this spell together, dab some honey on his or her chest and tongue.

5. You may choose to share an expression of love and forgiveness now, either to your partner directly (if he or she is participating in the spell with you) or to him or her in absentia. Know that your thoughts and feelings will be received.

6. Depending on the size of the candles you've chosen and the time frame you've allowed for conducting this spell, you may either snuff out the flames after a while or let the candles burn down completely. If you snuff them out before they've finished burning down, repeat the process the next day (or as soon as possible) to conclude the spell.

SALAMANDER SCRYING

Elementals are spirit beings that inhabit the four elements (earth, air, fire, and water). Salamanders serve as ambassadors from the element of fire. In her book *Practical Solitary Magic*, Nancy B. Watson explains, "Salamanders are the little ethereal creatures who animate the flame of a hearth fire or candle. They will help you achieve your fiery goals, and they will defend you as well." When you light the candle for this spell, you invite these spirits to join you as your accomplices.

Tools and Ingredients
A black candle in a holder
Matches or a lighter

1. Set the candle on your altar or another place where it can burn safely, and light it.
2. Gaze into the flame, allowing your focus to blur a little. Can you see tiny lizard-like entities dancing in the flame?
3. Continue looking at the flame and you may notice other images there too—you may even be able to see the future. This act of viewing distantly—observing things beyond your normal range of vision—is known as scrying.
4. Notice the feelings, impressions, insights, and other awarenesses that arise in your consciousness. Even if they don't mean anything to you now, they may be significant later. (Note them in your grimoire after you've finished scrying.)
5. Keep looking into the flame for as long as you like. When you're ready, extinguish the candle.

SPELL TO CALL A LOVER TO YOU

You can use this spell for at least two purposes: to attract a new lover or to end an estrangement and reconnect with a former lover. Begin this spell during the waxing moon, preferably when the sun and/or moon is in Libra, but at least three days before the full moon.

Tools and Ingredients

An object that represents your lover

An object that represents you

A white or gold taper or small pillar candle in a candleholder

A black or silver taper or small pillar candle in a candleholder

Matches or a lighter

1. Choose an object to represent your lover in this spell. It may be anything that reminds you of him or her, such as a tarot card, a crystal, a personal object, a photograph, or a figurine. Choose another object to represent you. Set these on your altar.

2. Stand the candles on your altar, with the white or gold candle (to represent day/sun) on the right and the black or silver one (to represent night/moon) on your left. The candles should be at least 1' apart. Position the objects you've chosen to represent you and your lover in front of the two candles.

3. Light the candles and gaze at the objects you've chosen to represent you and your lover. Allow loving feelings to arise in you. If you like, speak to your lover (aloud or in your mind) and express your hopes, desires, and intentions. When you begin to lose your focus, extinguish the candles.

4. The next day repeat this ritual, but move the candles and the symbolic objects a little closer together.

5. Continue performing this spell each day until the full moon or your lover appears. If you don't connect with your lover before the moon reaches its full phase, take a break until after the new moon and then begin the spell again.

WASH AWAY ROMANCE-KILLING STRESS

Responsibilities and stress in our daily lives can diminish the energy we have to enjoy romance with our primary partners. Ritual baths have long been part of magickal practice, designed to cleanse you of impurities from the outside world and shift you into a more peaceful place. Perform this spell alone or with your partner to emphasize your love and commitment and, well, make magick!

Tools and Ingredients

Pink Himalayan sea salt

Essential oil of ylang-ylang, jasmine, rose, or patchouli

4 pink or red votive candles (or floating candles)

Matches or a lighter

1. Draw a bath and sprinkle a handful of sea salt into the water. Water, as you know, represents the emotions, so this practice opens you to experience deeper feelings with your beloved. Salt acts as a purifier to disperse stress, impurities, and bad vibes. Himalayan salt is believed to contain many healthful properties—and pink is the color of love.

2. Add several drops of your preferred essential oil to the bathwater.

3. Place the candles at the corners of the bathtub, turn off the electric lights, and light the candles. If you're using floating candles, set them on the water.

4. Soak as long as it takes to relax fully—not just your muscles, but right down to the center of your being. Feel the worries and irritations of the day flowing away from you, into the bathwater.

5. When you feel peaceful and relaxed, emerge from your bath and towel off. As the bathwater flows down the drain, imagine it taking your tension and cares along with it, leaving you feeling refreshed in body, mind, and spirit.

6. If you wish, carry the candles into your bedroom; otherwise, extinguish the candles.

SPELL TO SEPARATE FROM A PAST PARTNER

Ending a partnership is often difficult, especially if one of the people involved doesn't really want the relationship to end. This spell helps smooth the transition so each of you can go on with your separate lives in peace. Begin this spell during the waning moon, at least three days before the new moon.

Tools and Ingredients

- 2 pillar candles (colors of your choice)
- A ballpoint pen, athame, nail, or other pointed tool
- Pine essential oil
- 2 candleholders
- A piece of citrine
- A piece of amber
- A piece of aquamarine
- Matches or a lighter

1. Designate one pillar candle to represent you and one to represent the person from whom you are separating. Choose colors that hold significance for you, perhaps related to your birth signs or favorite colors.

2. Engrave your initials in one candle and the other person's initials in the second candle.

3. Anoint both candles with pine essential oil and fit the candles in their holders, and then set them on your altar about 5" apart. The candle that represents you should be on the right and the candle that represents the other person should be on the left.

4. Place the citrine between the two candles to dissolve bonds and clear away old baggage. Position the amber below the citrine to provide protection. Place the aquamarine above the citrine for clarity and vision.

5. Light the candles and, as you watch them burn, send positive thoughts to your past partner to inspire peace between you. Aloud or mentally, affirm that the relationship has served its purpose and is now ended, with good to all concerned. Allow the candles to burn for at least ten minutes, and then snuff them out.

6. The next night, move the candles a few inches farther apart. Light the candles and spend at least ten minutes watching them burn as you send peaceful energy to your former partner. Snuff out the candles whenever you're ready.

7. On the third night move the candles farther apart, and then light them. Allow the candles to finish burning down completely.

8. The next morning, dispose of the candles in a barren place away from trees or water.

ASK THE ARCHANGEL GABRIEL FOR ASSISTANCE

West is the direction witches associate with the emotions and matters of the heart. The archangel Gabriel serves as guardian of the West, so you will be petitioning this deity's assistance via this spell. If possible, perform it while the moon is in Libra.

Tools and Ingredients

A blue candle

A ballpoint pen, athame, or other pointed tool

Essential oil of rose, ylang-ylang, jasmine, musk, or patchouli

A candleholder

Matches or a lighter

A flower, small vial of essential oil, or other token of thanks

1. Carve the rune Gebo (also called Gifu) on the candle with your pointed tool. This symbol looks like an X, a glyph we often associate with love or a kiss.

2. Dress the candle with the oil you've chosen (don't get it on the wick) and fit the candle into its holder.

3. Go to the westernmost part of your home (or your property, if you prefer to work outdoors) and place the candle there.

4. Light the candle and stand before it facing west. Feel peaceful, loving energy flowing toward you as you stare into the flame and say aloud:

"Angel Gabriel, guardian of the West,
Please hear my call and grant my request."

5. Relax and let your gaze soften as you look into the candle's flame. Can you see it transform into the figure of Gabriel wearing a blue robe? Speak to Gabriel openly and honestly. Ask for help in improving your love life. Ask for assistance in handling a problem you are experiencing. Ask for understanding, forgiveness, insight, strength—whatever you seek. Express yourself freely, knowing Gabriel will answer and offer aid.

6. Remain in communication with the archangel for as long as you like. When you sense that Gabriel has agreed to grant your request, give thanks. After the angel's shape fades, snuff out the candle.

7. Leave a token of thanks for Gabriel, such as a flower or a small vial of essential oil.

Candles in Dreams

It's not uncommon to see one or more candles in a dream. When you do, it could mean:

- Hope
- An awakening, idea, or insight
- Guidance
- The presence of Spirit or a guardian, angel, deity, etc.

FIRE SPELL TO ENCOURAGE FERTILITY

Fire represents the spark of life, creativity, and Spirit enlivening the material world. This spell draws upon an age-old practice engaged in by women who wished to become pregnant. However, you can also enact this spell to encourage the birth of children of the mind as well as of the body. Perform this spell alone or with other like-minded people. The best time to do this is on Imbolc (February 1–2); however, you can also do it when the moon is in Leo, the zodiac sign of creativity.

Tools and Ingredients

A cauldron or other large fireproof vessel

A large green pillar candle

Matches or a lighter

1. Set a cauldron or other large fireproof vessel in a place where you can safely light a flame and also have enough room for participants to jump over the cauldron. The cauldron represents the womb, and as such, signifies fertility.

2. Position the candle in the center of the cauldron and light it. A short, wide pillar is best for this spell because it's stable and less likely to ignite the clothing of someone who leaps over it. Green is the color of fertility and growth.

3. Invite the person (you or someone else) who seeks the gift of fertility to jump over the fire. Be careful to keep garments away from the flame. As you leap, envision the creative power of fire entering you and sparking your own creativity.

4. When you've finished, extinguish the candle. Give thanks for the blessing you've received, knowing that your intention will manifest.

The Modern Witchcraft Book of Love Spells

SPELL TO REUNITE WITH A LOST LOVE

It may seem that a relationship has ended—but perhaps, with a little magick, you can revive the love that once existed between you. Begin this spell during the waxing moon, at least three days before the full moon, preferably when the moon is in Libra. The candles that represent you and your former lover should either be of colors that correspond to your zodiac sun signs or colors that you and your lover particularly like. The candle that represents discord should be of a color you *don't* like.

Tools and Ingredients

A pink altar cloth

A candle to represent you, in a candleholder

A candle to represent a former lover, in a candleholder

A candle to represent discord, in a candleholder

Matches or a lighter

1. Spread the pink cloth on your altar.
2. Set the candle that represents you to the right and the one that represents the other person to the left, about 1' apart. Position the candle that represents discord between the other two.
3. Light the candles. Speak to your former love as if he or she were physically in the room with you. Describe your feelings for him or her and explain why you seek to rekindle the relationship. Also discuss the nature of the discord between you and your desire to remove the obstacle that's keeping you separated. If an apology is in order, offer it sincerely. Then extinguish the candles.
4. The next night, move the "discord" candle back a few inches and move the candles that represent you and the other person a few inches closer together. Light the candles and continue speaking to your intended lover, describing your wish to enjoy greater happiness together. Express

anything you would like to say to him or her personally that can heal the rift between you. Speak from your heart of loving, peaceful, joyous things—don't utter anger, resentment, ego demands, etc.

5. On the third night, move the "discord" candle to the back of the altar and move the other two candles closer together until they're touching. Light the candles and speak of how happy you are to be reunited with your lover. Promise to do your best to bring joy into the relationship. Sense your partner agreeing. If you sense he or she does not agree, accept this at least for the time being—other issues may be afoot that you don't know about.

6. Close with the words: "This is done in harmony with Divine Will, our own true wills, and with good to all concerned." Allow the candles to finish burning down completely.

POPPET CANDLE SPELL TO ENRICH YOUR RELATIONSHIP

According to a practice known as sympathetic magick, you can use an effigy to stand in for a person in a spell. This effigy is called a poppet. What you do to the poppet affects the person it represents. Often the poppet is a doll made of wax, cloth, wood, straw, or another material. You can fabricate your own candle poppets from wax for this spell (see the directions for the spell "Make a Magick Heart Candle" earlier in this chapter, or look online for candle-making instructions). If you prefer, you can purchase readymade candles shaped like humans.

This spell has many applications, depending on your intention. Do you want more passion and romance? Do you seek greater success and abundance through the relationship? Would you like more security, ease, and comfort? Determine your objective before you begin, because the steps in this spell are geared toward achieving your goal.

Tools and Ingredients

2 human-shaped candles

A ballpoint pen, athame, nail, or other pointed tool

Something representative of you: hair, fingernails, an article of clothing, etc.

Something representative of your partner: hair, fingernails, an article of clothing, etc.

Optional: melted wax from another source (not the human-shaped candles)

Essential oil associated with your intention (see chart in Chapter 4)

2 flame-resistant plates, ashtrays, or containers to hold the candles

Matches or a lighter

1. With the pen or other pointed tool, carve your name on one candle and your lover's name on the other.

2. Affix something representative of you to the poppet that bears your name—for example, snips of your hair or fingernails, and/or other personal items. You might consider dressing the poppet in your clothing, jewelry, etc. The objective is to symbolically link the wax poppet with you. If you opt to attach hair and/or fingernails bits to the poppet, sprinkle those in soft wax and stick the wax to the candle.

3. As you work, say aloud:

"Creature of wax, blessed be
What happens to you
Also happens to me."

4. Affix something that represents your lover to the poppet bearing his or her name. Again, it can be anything that carries his or her essence. The objective is to symbolically link the wax poppet with your beloved.

5. As you work, say aloud:

"Blessed be, creature of wax
Who stands in place

Of the one I love most.
I request your agreement
In enacting this spell.
May all we do here
Serve the greatest good.
May Divine Will be served
And may all be well."

6. Anoint the poppets with the essential oil(s) you've chosen. You can anoint both wax dolls with the same oil or use different oils—whatever seems appropriate for each of you and the circumstances.

7. Set the two poppets, in flame-resistant containers, on your altar or another place where you will be working. Light the candles.

8. Use the poppets to depict your intention(s). For example, if you seek a stronger bond between you and your partner, you might choose to tie a pink ribbon around the two wax figures to signify a bond. If you wish to increase the romantic love between you, lay a pink rose or piece of rose quartz between the poppet candles. If your goal is to work together for financial success, place a coin in front of the poppets.

9. Tell the poppet candles what you want them to do. Be as specific as you feel you need to be. You're actually guiding your inner self to accomplish your objectives.

10. When you've finished, extinguish the candles. Thank them, and then wrap them in a piece of silk and store them in a safe place until such time as you need to call on them again for assistance.

This spell is potentially manipulative, so to be on the safe side, end it with a disclaimer, such as: "This spell is done in harmony with Divine Will, our own true wills, and with good to all, harming none."

Chapter 3

SPELLCASTING WITH CRYSTALS AND GEMSTONES

Long before people began prizing gems for their monetary value, they used them as magick charms. In early societies only rulers, members of royal families, priests, and religious leaders wore gems. Today, adornment is the primary reason for wearing precious and semiprecious gems; however, a growing number of people (especially magick workers and healers) realize that crystals and gemstones have much more to offer us.

Each stone has unique properties and energies that you can tap in spellwork. As a general rule:

- Clear stones, such as diamonds and aquamarines, are best suited for dealing with mental/intellectual issues and communication.
- Translucent or cloudy stones, such as rose quartz, carnelians, and opals, aid emotional conditions, such as affection, anger, sadness, or passion.
- Opaque stones, such as agates and onyx, support physical matters, including sex and financial issues.

Witches also choose stones whose colors correspond to their intentions. In love spells, for example, pink and red stones are popular choices, though at times you may wish to include blue stones to encourage serenity, black stones for stability, or green stones for emotional healing. Gems may be used alone or in combination with other stones or crystals to facilitate the results you desire. The following table lists many gemstones and crystals witches use in love spells, along with the stones' individual properties.

CRYSTALS AND GEMS TO USE IN LOVE MAGICK	
Carnelian	To stimulate passion, sexual energy, courage, and initiative
Coral	To attract love or increase affectionate feelings; to enhance self-esteem; to calm emotions; to increase fertility
Diamond	To deepen commitment and trust in a love relationship
Emerald	To enhance love and devotion; to support emotional balance
Garnet	To bring luck in love; to enhance self-esteem
Hematite	To help stabilize emotions and encourage commitment in a relationship
Jade	To enhance beauty and health; to increase stability, loyalty, and joy in relationships
Malachite	To open your heart and increase your capacity to love
Moonstone	To make you more nurturing and accepting of others
Opal	To attract love and romance; to encourage harmony in relationships
Pearl	To strengthen self-esteem; to create balance in love relationships; to increase femininity

CRYSTALS AND GEMS TO USE IN LOVE MAGICK	
Red jasper	To stir up passion and improve sexual relations
Rose quartz	To attract love and friendship; to encourage emotional healing and harmony; to increase affection
Ruby	To stimulate the emotions, passion, and love; to open your heart to divine love
Turquoise	For emotional and physical healing, protection, happiness, and good fortune
Watermelon tourmaline	To increase your ability to give and receive love

Magick Birthstones

Birthstones resonate with the qualities of the zodiac signs to which they correspond. Originally people wore them to enhance, balance, or modulate their innate characteristics. When considering your birthstone, remember to look at the dates when the sun is positioned in a particular astrological sign—not the calendar month. For example, if you were born between about January 21 and February 19—when the sun is in Aquarius—your birthstone is garnet.

CARING FOR CRYSTALS AND GEMSTONES

Crystals and gemstones are intelligent beings that resonate at a different vibration than we do, and yet we can work with them for healing, magick, scrying, communication, meditation, astral travel, and other purposes. Each stone is as unique as each human being. You can connect with the special properties of crystals and gems to benefit you and others. Treat your stones with respect, as if they were good friends, and they'll serve you well for many years.

Cleansing Your Stones

Cleanse your crystals and gemstones regularly. It's easy: just hold them under running water or wash them with mild soap while you visualize them being purified by white light. Then let them sit in the sun to dry. This removes unwanted vibrations as well as dust. You can also clear crystals energetically by gently rubbing them with a piece of golden citrine.

It's a good idea to cleanse your stones before using them in a magick spell or ritual so ambient vibrations don't interfere with the purpose of your spell. You should also wash stones if they've been exposed to strong emotions or unsettling events.

Protect Your Gems

Some people recommend keeping stones in a silk, velvet, or linen bag, a wooden box, or another protected place when they're not in use. That's because crystals and gemstones retain ambient vibrations—especially those generated by people—which is why psychics can read a person by holding a piece of her favorite jewelry. Don't let anyone else touch the stones you use in magickal work.

Gemstone Sensing Exercise

Practice sensing the energies and resonances of crystals and gemstones before you start spellcasting. Choose several different stones. Close your eyes and pick up one. Hold it in your hand for several moments and notice any sensations or impressions you receive. You may feel slight tingling, warmth, or something else. Set down that stone and pick up another. Again, hold it and pay attention to anything you sense from it. Do different stones give off different vibes? Record your experiences in a journal or grimoire.

ROSE QUARTZ ATTRACTION SPELL

Quartz crystals amplify the energy you put into them—that's one reason witches prize them in spellcasting. Pretty pink rose quartz crystals are often linked with love and affection. The number two represents partnership.

Tools and Ingredients

2 rose quartz crystals (cleansed)

Rosewater (see Chapter 4)

1. Put the crystals in a place where the moon will shine on them overnight to imbue them with lunar energy (the moon governs emotions and witches connect it with the Goddess).

2. In the morning anoint the crystals with the rosewater potion.

3. Put a drop of rosewater on your chest near your heart.

4. Hold a crystal in each hand and close your eyes. Allow loving feelings to blossom in you. In your mind's eye send these feelings into the crystals. Continue this for a few minutes.

5. Hold the crystals to your lips. Speak directly to the crystals, asking them to help you attract the person who's right for you in every way.

6. When you feel ready, set the crystals on your bedside table, or, if you know feng shui, place them in your Relationship Gua.

"Our ancestors believed the Earth was surrounded by crystal spheres where gods, stars, and planets dwelt."

—JUDY HALL, *101 POWER CRYSTALS*

MAGICK GEMSTONE X

This spell combines the resonances of gemstones with the Norse rune for love, known as Gebo or Gifu. Notice the rune is also the symbol we use for a kiss. Choose nine gemstones from the table earlier in this chapter for this spell. Select any combination you wish—nine different stones, all the same, or whatever suits your purposes. Begin this spell nine days before the full moon.

Tools and Ingredients

9 gemstones of your choosing (cleansed)

1. Lay the stones in an X pattern on your altar (or another surface where you can leave the stones in place for nine days). As you put each one in place, say aloud how this stone will assist you. For example, if you've chosen a carnelian, you might say something like, "This carnelian now increases the passion in my love life."

2. When you've finished laying out the X, close your eyes and envision everything you want to manifest. Then open your eyes and say aloud, "So mote it be."

3. Leave the gemstone X in place for nine days, and then remove the stones. Thank them for their help, wash them, and store them in a safe place.

Love Stones in Nature

Any stone can become a magick token if you think of it in that way. Most likely you've picked up pretty stones from special places you've visited and brought them home as mementos. They already hold meaning for you, so all you need do is project your intentions into them. Heart-shaped stones or stones with heart-shaped inclusions are ideal to use as love stones.

GODDESS GEMSTONE SPELL

Mythology, folklore, and magick link several goddesses with love—Venus, Aphrodite, Freya, and Hathor are among the best known. Do you feel a special kinship with one of these deities, or another goddess? With this spell you invite her to assist you in matters of the heart. According to some spiritual traditions, burning incense imbues the figure of the deity with life. Perform this spell on a Friday.

Tools and Ingredients

An image of a love goddess (a figurine, painting, picture downloaded from the Internet, etc.)

A stick or cone of incense in a holder (rose, jasmine, gardenia, ylang-ylang, patchouli, or musk)

Matches or a lighter

A gemstone associated with love, cleansed (see the table in this chapter for suggestions)

1. Set the image of the goddess on your altar or other place where you will do this spell.

2. Place the incense next to the goddess image and light it.

3. Gaze at the image of the goddess and feel a loving connection with her. Allow your heart and mind to open, knowing she will assist you.

4. Ask the goddess for guidance and help with a matter of the heart. Then place the gemstone before her as an offering. When you sense the goddess has agreed to aid you, thank her with a prayer or blessing.

5. Allow the incense to finish burning. Carry the gemstone with you to continue bringing aid.

ADORN A MAGICK WAND WITH GEMS

You can purchase a beautiful magick wand emblazoned with gemstones—or you can make your own. Because the wand is considered a tool of masculine energy (the phallic symbolism is obvious), it's best to craft your wand when the sun and/or moon is in a fire sign: Aries, Leo, or Sagittarius. Make sure to cleanse the crystal and gemstones before assembling your wand.

Tools and Ingredients

A quartz single-terminated crystal (this means it has one point), cleansed

A wooden rod, at least 6" in length

Fine wire

Gemstones of your choice, cleansed (see the table earlier in this chapter for suggestions)

Optional: ribbons, feathers, or other decorations of your choice

1. Fasten the crystal to the end of the rod with wire, forming a pointed tip.
2. Arrange the gemstones along the rod in whatever configuration pleases you, and then fasten them to your wand with more wire. You may need to form tiny wire "baskets" to hold the gemstones. If you possess jewelry-making skill, you can set the gemstones in metal. Slide brass or iron bands around the wand, and then affix the gems to the bands.
3. If you like, add any other decorations that appeal to you: ribbons, feathers, etc.
4. Charge and consecrate your wand according to whatever method you choose.
5. To draw love to you, cast a circle so that you are inside it. Point the wand toward the heavens and visualize loving energy flowing down through the wand, into your arm, and finally into your heart. When you feel suffused with love, lower the wand and open the circle.

CRYSTAL COMMITMENT SPELL

Do you feel it's time to move your relationship to a deeper, more serious level? Is one (or both) of you commitment-shy? Perform this spell when the moon is in Capricorn, the sign of longevity and stability.

Tools and Ingredients

A stick of pine incense in a holder

Matches or a lighter

2 clear quartz crystals with flat bottoms (cleansed)

A piece of dark pink ribbon, long enough to tie together the two crystals

1. Place the incense in its holder on your altar and light it. Take a few moments to enjoy the fresh, clean scent. Witches associate pine with endurance—think of the pine tree that holds onto its needles even during winter.

2. Hold the crystals in the incense smoke for a few moments to charge them while you say the following incantation aloud (or compose your own):

> *"I love you and you love me*
> *Together we shall always be.*
> *Every night and every day*
> *Happiness is here to stay."*

3. Set the crystals side by side on your altar (or another spot where you can leave them in place for at least a week). Tie them together with the ribbon, making eight knots.

4. While the incense finishes burning, envision your love growing stronger and your joy blossoming.

5. Allow the crystals to stay in place for at least a week or longer if you choose.

HEART-HEALING SPELL

We've all suffered the pain of a broken heart. This spell uses a red-and-green stone known as ruby zoisite to help soothe the ache. The chain for the pendant necklace in this spell should be long enough to let the stone hang at the center of your heart. The stone needn't be large, but make sure it hasn't been pierced (that can destroy its power). Bleeding heart flower essence is available online or in health food stores.

Tools and Ingredients

Bleeding heart flower essence

A pendant necklace set with a ruby zoisite (cleansed)

A green candle in a holder

Matches or a lighter

1. Put a couple of drops of bleeding heart flower essence under your tongue, and then rub some on the ruby zoisite.

2. Slip the chain over your head and feel the stone lying against your heart center.

3. Light the candle and gaze into the flame. Breathe slowly and deeply, allowing your mind to grow calm. As you inhale, feel the love of the Goddess entering you. As you exhale, feel pain and sadness flowing away from you.

4. Continue until you feel some relief or your attention starts to wander. Extinguish the candle.

5. Repeat the meditation at least once a day, or as often as you feel the need. Wear the ruby zoisite pendant until the pain eases, or as long as you like.

PENDULUM MAGICK

When you need advice about a romantic matter, a pendulum can help you get answers quickly. Using a pendulum to gain insight is an ancient dowsing technique that dates back thousands of years.

Tools and Ingredients

A pendulum with a crystal or gemstone point (or "bob"), cleansed
A piece of silk or a velvet or silk pouch (to store the pendulum)

1. Calm and center yourself. Loosely hold the pendulum by the chain (or cord) so the stone hangs a few inches above your altar's surface or a tabletop.

2. Ask a question that can be answered with a "yes" or "no" response.

3. After a bit, the pendulum will begin moving of its own accord—don't try to influence its motion intentionally. If the pendulum swings from side to side, the answer is "no." If it swings back and forth (toward you and then away from you), the answer is "yes." If it swings in a clockwise circle, the situation supports your intention. If it moves in a counterclockwise circle, the situation doesn't support your intention at this time.

4. If you want to ask another question, stop the pendulum first, and then repeat the process.

5. When you've finished, thank the pendulum for its assistance. Wrap it in a piece of silk or slip it into a silk or velvet pouch and store it in a safe place.

"You can only learn to use a pendulum by practicing with it regularly. As with any divination tool, it takes a lot of practice to become proficient and reliable with the pendulum. However, pendulum divining is the easiest and fastest of all divining methods to learn."

—D.J. Conway, *A Little Book of Pendulum Magic*

BOOST YOUR LOVE QUOTIENT

Do you feel less desirable than you'd like to be? Do you find it hard to express loving feelings? This spell lets you draw upon the powers of the sun and moon to enhance your love quotient. Witches connect the sun with the God and masculine energy, the moon with the Goddess and feminine energy. If possible perform this spell during a full moon.

Tools and Ingredients

A quartz crystal with a single point (cleansed)

1. Hold the crystal to your "third eye" (the center of psychic ability, on your forehead between your eyebrows) and project a vision of love, beauty, and happiness into the crystal.
2. At dawn, set the crystal on a windowsill where the sun can shine on it during the day and the moon during the night. Make sure the point aims into your home.
3. State your intention or request aloud, in the form of an affirmation.
4. The next morning remove the crystal from the windowsill and hold it to your heart. Feel the solar and lunar vibrations flowing into you, infusing you with the light and love of the Goddess and the God. Thank the sun and moon and the crystal for their assistance.
5. Carry the crystal with you during the day and set it on your bedside table (or under your pillow) at night.

A Drink Fit for a Queen

According to legend, Cleopatra drank a mixture of crushed pearls and vinegar to attract love and increase her sex appeal.

MOONSTONE DREAM COMMUNICATION

Some people believe we can communicate with others via our dreams. When we're relaxed and our minds are open, we can access higher levels of consciousness. This easy spell helps you share messages with a lover while you sleep. If you're seeking a new partner, send your intention in your dreams.

Tools and Ingredients

A moonstone (cleansed)
Rosewater (see Chapter 4)

1. Sit quietly in your bedroom, close your eyes, and hold the moonstone to your "third eye" (the center of psychic ability, on your forehead between your eyebrows).
2. Think loving thoughts; visualize those thoughts being absorbed by the moonstone.
3. Open your eyes and anoint the moonstone with the rosewater.
4. Place the gemstone under your pillow while you sleep; it will project your loving thoughts to your partner during the night.

"The diamond and other precious stones are focuses of light, and essences of colour which seem expressly created to ornament on a small scale the human body with all the splendours which adorn the universe on a large scale."

—CHARLES BLANC, *ART IN ORNAMENT AND DRESS*

SPELL TO STRENGTHEN SELF-LOVE

Before you can enjoy a fulfilling, loving relationship with someone else, you have to love yourself and feel you deserve to be loved by another person. This spell taps the energies of several gemstones to balance your emotions and strengthen your self-esteem. The stones needn't be large, and if you wish to include other stones too that's fine. (See the table earlier in the chapter for suggestions, or let yourself be drawn to stones that "speak" to you.) Be sure to cleanse all the stones before you begin the spell.

Tools and Ingredients

3 pieces of rose quartz

3 pieces of alexandrite

3 pieces of garnet

3 pieces of chrysocolla

3 pieces of opal

3 pieces of jade

1. Cast a circle around yourself by laying the stones on the floor or ground so that you are inside the circle. Start in the east and work in a clockwise direction. You can position the stones in any order you like.

2. Sit in the center of the circle and close your eyes.

3. Breathe slowly and deeply, feeling the positive energies of the stones flowing toward you. Accept the blessings they offer for your highest and most joyful good.

4. Sit this way for as long as you like, and then pick up the stones in a counterclockwise direction to open the circle. Thank the stones and store them in a safe place until you choose to do this spell again.

GEMSTONE STABILITY SPELL

Has your relationship been a bit rocky lately? The gemstones in this spell help detox negative energy and "ground" tension, to bring greater stability to your relationship. If you wish, you can perform this spell with your partner.

Tools and Ingredients

4 pieces of onyx, at least the size of a walnut (cleansed)
4 pieces of watermelon tourmaline, at least the size of a walnut (cleansed)
Essential oil of pine

1. Anoint each stone with a dab of pine essential oil.
2. Place one onyx and one watermelon tourmaline in each corner of your bedroom. Begin at the easternmost corner and move in a clockwise direction around the room. If you know feng shui, you can do this in the Relationship Gua of your home instead (your choice).
3. When you've finished, stand in the center of the room, facing west. Hold your arms straight out at your sides, so that your body forms a cross, with your right palm turned up and your left palm turned down.
4. Call upon the archangel Gabriel, whom witches associate with the element of water, emotions, and relationships. Speak the following incantation or compose one of your own:

> *"Archangel Gabriel, I seek your aid*
> *Help us be patient, kind, and true.*
> *Let us love and respect one another*
> *In all that we think, say, and do."*

5. Thank Gabriel for assisting you. Leave the gemstones in place to continue keeping your relationship on an even keel.

SPELL TO END AN UNWANTED RELATIONSHIP

Ending a relationship can be difficult, but this spell helps you ease the transition. Perform the spell during the waning moon for best results.

Tools and Ingredients

3 votive candles, 1 black, 1 white, and 1 light blue

1 piece of clear quartz

1 piece of chrysocolla

1 piece of watermelon tourmaline

1 piece of obsidian

A terra cotta bowl

Matches or a lighter

A small piece of paper

A pen that writes blue ink

1. Set the candles on your altar (or other surface) in a triangular configuration with the point facing away from you. Set the black candle at the bottom left angle, the blue one at the bottom right, and the white one at the apex of the triangle.

2. Place the gemstones in a square configuration within the triangle. Arrange them in whatever order feels right to you.

3. Place the bowl in the center of the gemstone square.

4. Light the candles.

5. On the piece of paper, write the following affirmation (or compose one of your own): "I now release you [person's name] to go your way as I go mine. Thanks be to you for all the good things we shared and all we learned from each other. Let there be peace between us, now and always."

6. Hold the paper over the bowl; light it and drop it into the bowl. State the affirmation aloud three times as the paper burns. Envision the other person leaving your life as you visualize yourself surrounded by a ball of pure white light.

7. Allow the candles to finish burning. Leave the gemstones in place overnight, and then in the morning wash them and store them in a safe place.

The Modern Witchcraft Book of Love Spells

ASK THE RUNES FOR LOVE ADVICE

The runes with which most people are familiar come from early Norse culture. According to mythology, the god Odin brought the magick of the runes to humankind. Each letter in this ancient alphabet represents an animal, object, condition, or deity. You can use the runes as an oracle to gain advice, understand the hidden dynamics of a situation, or see the future. They also play a part in many spells, such as this one. You can purchase a readymade set of rune stones—they're available in a lot of different gems (amethyst, rose quartz, turquoise, onyx, etc.). Or, you can acquire the tumbled stones and then paint the glyphs on them yourself.

Tools and Ingredients

A set of rune stones

Optional: a book that explains the meanings of the individual runes (you can also find information about runes online)

1. Sit quietly, calm your mind, and think of a question you want answered or a situation into which you seek insight.

2. With your hands, mix up the stones—without looking at them. Contemplate your question or concern, then express it aloud. For example, you might ask, "How can I improve my relationship with [partner's name]?"

3. Select a single stone. If you don't already know the meanings of the different runes, take a moment to let your intuition send you impressions before looking up the interpretation in a book or online.

4. If you don't understand the guidance you've been given, you can ask for additional insight and then draw another stone. But if you just don't like the answer, don't pull another rune stone and hope it will give you a more favorable take on the situation.

5. You can do more complex readings with runes, laying them out in patterns as you would tarot cards. In fact, the same "spreads" you use in tarot are suitable for rune readings. (For an explanation of some of these spreads, see my *The Modern Witchcraft Book of Tarot.*) Here's an easy spread: Select one rune to represent the past conditions surrounding your question or concern, and lay it on your altar or a table. Choose a second rune stone to signify the present situation, and lay it to the right of the first stone. Draw a third stone to show what the future is likely to bring, and lay it to the right of the "present" stone. Spend a few minutes gazing at the stones, allowing the symbols to convey insights to you. Then write down the reading in a journal or grimoire.

6. When you've finished, thank the runes and store them in a cloth pouch for safekeeping until you decide to do another reading. The more often you work with your rune stones, the better you'll get at interpreting them.

Gnome Magick

Gnomes are elemental beings that most people can't see, but these little fellows can help you if you ask. As "ambassadors" of the earth element, gnomes are well suited to assist you in physical areas, such as enhancing your sex life or protecting a loved one. You must offer a gift to a gnome who aids you; otherwise he may play a trick on you instead. Gnomes are fond of crystals and gemstones, so give your elemental helper one as a thank-you present.

CRYSTAL BALL SCRYING

When you think of seeing into the future, perhaps an image of a turbaned gypsy gazing into a crystal ball comes to mind. Although that image is a cliché, you really can glimpse things beyond your normal range of vision by looking into a crystal ball; the technique is known as scrying. Be sure to cleanse your crystal ball before beginning to scry.

Tools and Ingredients

A genuine crystal ball (not a glass substitute)

A white candle in a candleholder

Matches or a lighter

1. Hold your crystal ball in both hands while you calm and center yourself. Breathe slowly and deeply, hold the ball near your solar plexus, and allow yourself to make a connection with the crystal.

2. When you feel ready, set the candle on your altar and light it.

3. Depending on the size of your crystal ball, you may choose to hold it as you scry or, alternately, to position it on your altar. Some people like to set their balls on light boxes that illuminate the many intricate features within crystal balls.

4. If you have a specific intention, state it aloud now.

5. Allow your mind to relax as you focus your attention on the crystal ball. You'll notice a lot of cloudy wisps, veins, rainbows, silvery "plates," and other features within the crystal. Let yourself be drawn to those that intrigue you. For instance, you may notice a "hole" or "tunnel" inside the crystal ball, and long to see where it leads—follow it with your imagination.

6. The silvery plates, which may look like tiny mirrors or slivers of aluminum foil, are magick tablets on which you can lay out your intentions. If you spot one in your crystal ball, imagine writing your wishes and objectives on it.

7. Most likely, you'll start seeing lights, shadows, images, and more within your crystal ball. You may even witness entire scenarios unfolding before you. Observe them, as they may provide answers or information.

8. Continue scrying with your crystal ball for as long as you like. When you start to feel tired or your attention begins to wander, stop.

9. Thank the crystal ball and whatever guides, angels, or spirits have assisted you. Record in your journal or grimoire what you saw and experienced.

SPELLCASTING WITH CRYSTAL SINGING BOWLS

Singing bowls resonate with beautiful sounds when tapped or stroked with a mallet. For hundreds of years, they've been used for meditation, relaxation, sound healing, and rites, but you can also work magick with them. Many are made of bronze; however you can also purchase crystal singing bowls. Some are made of different types of crystal and toned to correspond to various chakras.

Tools and Ingredients

1 or more crystal singing bowls, cleansed

A rubber stand or cushion

A padded mallet

1. Set the singing bowl on the stand or cushion.

2. Stand or sit before it in a comfortable position. State your intention aloud, for example, to attract new love or to improve an existing relationship.

3. Hold the mallet in your hand and gently stroke the rim of the bowl with it, causing it to "sing." Gently tap the side of the bowl. As the sound fills the room, it carries your intention with it and amplifies it.

4. Continue playing as long as you wish. When you've finished, thank the bowl and whatever guides, angels, or spirits have assisted you. Store the bowl in a safe place.

Charging and Consecrating Your Magick Tools

Many witches charge and consecrate their tools before using them. Until you imbue your wand with energy and purpose, it's just an ordinary rod. This process may involve a complex ritual, or you may simply say something like, "I now consecrate this wand to do the work of the Goddess and charge it to assist me in my magickal practice, in harmony with Divine Will, my own true will, and for the good of all concerned."

Chapter 4

PLANT MAGICK

According to Greek myth, the daughters of the goddess Hecate (one of the patronesses of witchcraft) taught witches how to use plants for both healing and magick—and so it has been ever since. Greek mythology also tells us that a nymph named Chloris (her Roman name was Flora) turned a number of characters into flowers, including Crocus, Narcissus, and Hyacinthus.

Flowers play an important role in matters of the heart. We give flowers on Valentine's Day to express love and happiness. A new bride tosses her wedding bouquet to bring luck in love to the woman who catches it. In this chapter you'll find spells that call upon the magickal properties of a variety of botanicals: flowers, herbs and spices, essential oils, and trees.

FLOWERS TO USE IN LOVE SPELLS	
Carnation	For good luck, healing, and longevity in love
Daffodil	For fertility, happiness, and luck in love
Daisy	To encourage flirtation, fun, and cheerfulness
Gardenia	For emotional healing, tranquility, and harmony
Hyacinth	For happiness and protection in love

FLOWERS TO USE IN LOVE SPELLS	
Iris	To inspire harmony and cooperation in a relationship
Jasmine	For seduction and sensual pleasure
Lavender	To restore peace and dissolve hard feelings after a disagreement
Myrtle	Keeps love alive and promotes peace
Pansy	To soothe the heart after a loss
Primrose	To spark new love and passion
Rose	For all love spells; red stimulates passion, pink inspires romance and affection, white supports spiritual connection
Tulip	Attracts and nurtures abundance in a relationship
Violet	Encourages fertility, prosperity, and peace

East Meets West

During the clipper ship era of the nineteenth century, trade expanded between Asia, Europe, and the United States. Spices from the East were valuable imports, prized not only as culinary seasonings but also as magickal aids. Ginseng was one of the treasured herbs brought from China, and healers today still associate it with beneficial properties, perhaps (as sympathetic magick would say) because the root looks like a human body.

HERBAL MAGICK

Throughout history witches have practiced herbalism, for healing purposes as well as magickal ones. You can probably find the basic herbs you need for spells in any large supermarket, farmers' market, or health food store; however, the most potent botanicals are those you grow yourself. If possible, grow a few favorite herbs in a kitchen garden or containers so you have them at the ready whenever you need them for a spell. The following table lists numerous botanicals that can benefit love spells, but don't hesitate to investigate further—you'll discover a treasure trove of information about plant magick that taps the powers of the tiniest herb to the tallest tree.

HERBS AND SPICES TO USE IN LOVE SPELLS	
Allspice	Attracts good fortune through love and relationships
Cacao	Adds sweetness and richness to a relationship
Cayenne	Increases passion and excitement
Chamomile	Calms stressful situations and restores balance after a time of upset
Cinnamon	Stimulates vitality and passion
Ginger	Boosts the power of any spell and speeds results
Marjoram	Attracts happiness and blessings, especially in a new partnership
Rosemary	Promotes fidelity and harmony
Sage	Purifies any space or object, dispels hard feelings
Vanilla	Brings joy and lightheartedness in a relationship

MAGICK ROSEWATER

You can use this versatile and fragrant flower water in many magickal ways: to anoint candles and gemstones, to add to bathwater, and to sprinkle on talismans. You can even rub it on your skin. Several spells in this book call for this magick potion, so you'll want to make it often. Perform this spell in the evening, preferably when the moon is in Taurus or Libra.

Tools and Ingredients

A glass, copper, or ceramic bowl (without any images on it)

Spring water (enough to fill the glass bottle)

Red or pink rose petals, as many as you like (preferably from wild-crafted or organically grown roses)

Rose essential oil

A silver or silver-plated spoon

A glass bottle (clear or green, without any images on it) with a cap or stopper

1. Fill the bowl with spring water.

2. Scatter the rose petals on the water. Set the bowl in the moonlight overnight so the water can absorb the loving energy of the moon.

3. In the morning, strain out the rose petals and set them aside for future spells.

4. Add a few drops of rose essential oil and stir in a clockwise direction, making three complete circles. As you stir, project loving thoughts into the water.

5. Pour the water into the bottle and cap it. Shake it three times before each use. Store it in a cool, dark place.

Bach Flower Remedies

In the 1920s and 1930s, English physician Dr. Edward Bach created a system of healing with flower remedies that's still popular today. To make the remedies, Bach floated flowers in bowls of water and left them to sit in sunlight for three hours, to allow the energy of the flowers to be imparted to the water.

FLORAL DREAM PILLOW

Make this fragrant floral sachet and put it under your pillow at night to bring sweet dreams. It can also help promote peaceful feelings in a romantic relationship.

Tools and Ingredients

A piece of pink cloth, at least
    3" × 6"

A needle and pink thread

Dried lavender flowers

Dried pink rose petals

Dried myrtle flowers

Dried violets

1. Fold the piece of cloth in half and sew two sides together.
2. Fill the cloth with dried flowers, and then stitch the third side closed. Sleep with the floral pillow beside your regular pillow at night.

Fresh Flowers or Dried?

The flower of a plant carries a tidy bundle of energy, for it is the sexual organ of the plant, how the plant reproduces. Do dried flowers carry a different energy than that of fresh flowers? Yes and no; the intrinsic energy remains, but its expression is different. For certain rituals or charms you may want the vibrancy of fresh flowers, whereas for other charms, such as sachets or powders, you may prefer dried flowers, which tend to exhibit a slower, longer-lasting energy.

PLANT A ROMANTIC GARDEN

Encourage romance by planting flowers associated with love (see the table earlier in this chapter for suggestions). If you don't have a place to grow them outdoors, you can plant small varieties in flowerpots. Plant your romantic garden during the waxing moon, preferably when the sun and/or moon is in Taurus or Libra. Choose red or pink flowering varieties, if possible.

Tools and Ingredients

A trowel

Potting soil (if you're planting in containers)

Flowerpots or other containers (unless you can plant directly in the ground)

Flowers of your choice

Water

1. If you're using containers, spoon potting soil into the flowerpots. Or, dig holes directly in the ground if you're planting outside.

2. Settle the plants in the soil and then water them. While you work, think loving thoughts.

3. Care for your flowers with devotion—talk to them, play music for them, feed, water, weed, and prune them. The attention you lavish on them symbolizes the care you give to your relationship. As they grow strong and healthy, so will your love.

Floral Love Letters

During Victorian times, a language of flowers evolved; each flower was assigned a certain meaning. This enabled suitors to send bouquets to their sweethearts as "love letters," which conveyed intentions in a beautiful way.

EASY ROSE ATTRACTION SPELL

Quartz crystals hold and amplify the energies with which they come in contact. Don't discount this spell because it's so easy—it's both pleasing and powerful. Perform this spell during the waxing moon, preferably when the moon is in Taurus or Libra.

Tools and Ingredients

A small bowl, heart-shaped if possible

Dried pink or red rose petals (enough to fill the bowl)

A clear quartz crystal (cleansed)

1. Fill the bowl with dried rose petals.
2. Nestle the quartz crystal in the rose petals. Set the bowl on a windowsill or other spot where the moon can shine on the crystal overnight and imbue it with her loving energy.
3. In the morning, remove the crystal from its bed of roses. Scatter the rose petals in front of your home.
4. Carry the crystal with you to attract love.

SPELL TO DRAW LOVE TO YOUR HOME

Sometimes the best spells are simple ones that draw upon our customs and familiar practices. This one also uses universal symbolism to engage your creative power and attract love. Circles represent harmony, unity, and wholeness; thus the practice of hanging a circular wreath on the door to your home is a symbolic, magickal act that draws these conditions to you.

Tools and Ingredients

A circular wreath form (buy one or make your own)

Greenery and flowers that represent your desires (see the table earlier in this chapter)

1. Fashion or acquire a circular wreath form.
2. Attach dried or fresh flowers and greenery to the form. Hang the wreath on the door to your home to attract love and happiness.

MAKE A ROMANTIC POTPOURRI

The botanicals in this fragrant blend serve two purposes: They bring pleasing scents into your home and they lend magickal energies to bless your love. Do this spell on a Friday, during the waxing moon to attract or increase romance.

Tools and Ingredients

A pink or red bowl, preferably a heart-shaped one

Dried red or pink rose petals

Dried red or pink carnation petals

Dried rosemary

Cinnamon sticks

Dried grated orange rind

Whole cloves

1. In the bowl combine all flowers and spices while you think loving thoughts. The amounts you use depend on what smells good to you and the size of the bowl.
2. Set the bowl on your nightstand or your altar. If you know feng shui, you can place it in the Relationship Gua of your home.
3. When you notice the scent starts to diminish, make a fresh batch of potpourri to keep your romance sweet and spicy.

The Modern Witchcraft Book of Love Spells

ADD SPICE TO YOUR LOVE LIFE

Has the spark gone out of your relationship? This spell uses spices to add spice to your love life, along with fire to heat up things between you and your partner. Perform this spell during the waxing moon, preferably on a Tuesday.

Tools and Ingredients

A cauldron (or fireproof pot)

Kindling (from one or more of the sacred trees, if possible)

Matches or a lighter

Ground cinnamon

Ground cayenne pepper

Dry mustard

Ground ginger

An envelope

1. Set your cauldron in a place where you can burn a small fire safely.
2. Put the kindling in the cauldron and light the kindling.
3. Sprinkle the dried spices in the fire while visualizing you and your lover in a passionate embrace.
4. When the fire has finished burning, allow the ashes to cool. Put the cooled ashes in an envelope and place it on your nightstand or under your bed.

Sacred Trees

The Celts considered certain trees sacred and believed they held magickal properties. Burning the wood from these trees in a ritual fire could bring good fortune, protection, love, and other blessings. Among the sacred trees are alder, apple, ash, birch, blackthorn, cedar, elder, elm, fir, hawthorn, hazel, holly, oak, pine, rowan, willow, and yew.

MAKE YOUR OWN OGHAM RUNES

The early Celts used an alphabet called Ogham, based on trees. Each of the twenty letters, or runes, in the Ogham alphabet has a central vertical "trunk" with horizontal or diagonal "branches" sprouting from it. Like Norse runes, Ogham runes can be used as an oracle to answer questions about love. You can make your own set of runes from the branch of a sacred tree. (You can find a table of the Ogham letters in my book *The Modern Witchcraft Grimoire* or online.)

Tools and Ingredients

A small tree branch

A handsaw

Sandpaper

Pink or red paint (or nail polish)

1. Choose a tree and ask its permission to cut a small branch from it. Thank the tree and leave an offering for it in return for its branch.
2. Cut the branch into twenty small circles; sand the circles smooth.
3. Paint one rune symbol on each circle.
4. When the paint dries, cast the runes to gain insight and guidance. Store your runes in a safe place when not in use.

"How much I can learn from a tree! The tree is my church, the tree is my temple, the tree is my mantra, the tree is my poem and my prayer."

—Satish Kumar, *No Destination*

GARDEN CHARM TO PROTECT LOVE

Unlike amulets and talismans, a garden charm is hung outside, preferably from a sacred tree. It's intended to disintegrate over time, releasing its contents to the earth. Witches often fashion these charms to protect property, but you can make this one to protect your relationship and foster happiness.

Tools and Ingredients

A white (or unbleached) cotton drawstring pouch, large enough to hold all the materials

Dried rose petals

Dried lavender flowers

Sunflower seeds

Dried carnation petals

A sprig of rosemary

A pinch of allspice

Dried basil leaves

1. Fill the pouch with the plant material and tie it closed, making three knots.

2. Tie the pouch to the twig of a tree (ask the tree's permission first). Say the following incantation aloud, or compose one of your own:

> *"With the Goddess's grace from above*
> *And the help of this sacred tree*
> *This magick charm protects our love*
> *And we shall always happy be."*

3. Gradually, the pouch will decompose and release the botanicals inside. As this happens, the charm reinforces your intention and nurtures your relationship.

SPELL TO HELP LOVE GROW STRONG

This spell taps a tree's strength to help your love grow strong. Because trees live a long time, their energy can also support longevity in your relationship.

Tools and Ingredients

A small wooden box

Red or pink rose petals

Red or pink carnation petals

A pinch of allspice

A sprig of rosemary

A small silver heart charm

A piece of onyx

A piece of rose quartz

A shovel

Rosewater (see the spell in this chapter)

1. Open the wooden box and place the botanicals, silver heart, and gemstones inside. As you add each ingredient, think about how it will contribute to your love and support your relationship.

2. Close the box and go outside, taking the shovel and rosewater with you.

3. Choose a healthy, mature tree and ask it to lend its energy to your spell. When you sense its agreement, dig a hole nearby and bury the box in it.

4. Thank the tree for its assistance and pour the rosewater at its base to show your gratitude.

Tree Attunement Exercise

Pick a tree. Hold one hand about 1" away from the bark and sense the energy of the tree. Then touch the bark. Explore how the tree feels to your hands. Bend close and smell the tree. Close your eyes and listen to the sounds the tree makes in response to the environment. Look closely at the tree and observe the different textures, colors, and markings. Caress its leaves. If it has fruit and you know it to be safe, taste it. Do this exercise with different kinds of trees. Compare and contrast your experiences.

SPELL FOR FORGIVENESS

Has your lover done something you find hurtful? Are you having trouble forgiving him or her? This spell softens hard feelings so you can release the pain and find peace again. You can also adapt this spell to forgive yourself.

Tools and Ingredients

A piece of pink paper

A pen or marker that writes blue ink

Vanilla essential oil

A cauldron

Kindling (preferably from a sacred tree)

Matches or a lighter

Hyacinth flowers

1. On the paper, write a message to your lover that expresses your intention to forgive him or her so that your relationship can continue happily. Forgiveness isn't the same as condoning an action, but unless you can forgive and let go, you'll keep on suffering.

2. When you've finished, dot each corner of the paper with vanilla essential oil. Inhale the soothing fragrance as you allow your mind to grow calm, your heart to grow peaceful.

3. Set your cauldron in a place where you can burn a small fire safely. Put the kindling in the cauldron.

4. Light the kindling and drop the paper into the fire. As it burns, allow all hard feelings to disintegrate too. Drop the hyacinth flowers into the flame.

5. When the paper and flowers have burned completely, scatter the ashes to symbolically release the hurt and free you to find joy again.

CAST A CIRCLE WITH INCENSE

With this easy technique you accomplish two things simultaneously: You cast a circle within which to perform a spell or ritual, and you purify the sacred space with smoke.

Tools and Ingredients

4 sticks or cones of sandalwood incense in holders
Matches or a lighter

1. Position one stick or cone of incense in a holder at each of the four compass directions in the space where you will work your magick.

2. Beginning at the east, light the incense and call out to the entity who guards that direction:

> *"Guardian of the eastern sphere*
> *Now I seek your presence here.*
> *Come, East, come and be near."*

3. Walk in a clockwise direction to the south; light the incense and call out to the entity who guards that direction:

> *"Guardian of the southern sphere*
> *Now I seek your presence here.*
> *Come, South, come and be near."*

4. Continue walking in a clockwise direction to the west; light the incense and call out to the entity who guards that direction:

> *"Guardian of the western sphere*
> *Now I seek your presence here.*
> *Come, West, come and be near."*

5. Walk in a clockwise direction to the north; light the incense and call out to the entity who guards that direction:

"Guardian of the northern sphere
Now I seek your presence here.
Come, North, come and be near."

Now you're ready to enact your spell or ritual within the circle of incense.

BURN INCENSE TO CLEANSE SACRED SPACE

For centuries temples and churches have burned incense to cleanse sacred space. You can burn incense to clear bad vibes from a space in which you want to do a spell or ritual. After an argument or upsetting experience, it's a good idea to cleanse the space too. Sage is the herb most often used for this purpose, but you can burn pine, frankincense, sandalwood, eucalyptus, or another scent if you prefer.

Tools and Ingredients

Incense (stick, cone, or coil)   Matches or a lighter
An incense holder   A large feather

1. Fit the incense into the holder and light the incense.
2. Carry the incense in its holder around the space you wish to cleanse, letting its fragrant smoke waft about the area.
3. Fan the smoke with the feather to direct the smoke where you want it to go, to remove any unwanted vibrations.

PURIFY MAGICK OBJECTS WITH INCENSE

It's a good idea to cleanse all objects before you use them in love spells, but in some cases you don't want to do this with soap and water. Incense, then, is the way to go.

Tools and Ingredients

Incense (sage, pine, frankincense, sandalwood, or another scent you prefer)

An incense holder

Matches or a lighter

1. Fit the incense into the holder and light the incense.
2. Hold the object in the incense smoke for a minute or so while you envision the object being cleansed and cleared of all unwanted resonances.

BATH SALTS TO INCREASE LOVE

You can make your own bath salts to boost the power of an herbal bath. Feel free to experiment with various essential oils to discover which ones you like best and which best serve your purposes.

Tools and Ingredients

2 cups sea salt or Epsom salt

A clear glass jar with a lid

2 drops jasmine essential oil

2 drops orange essential oil

2 drops cinnamon essential oil

1. Pour the salts into the jar.
2. Add the essential oils; cap the jar and shake it to combine. Think loving thoughts as you work, projecting them into the salt mixture.
3. Add a handful of the fragrant salts to bathwater. Between baths, store the salts in a cool, dark place.

Chapter 5

TALISMANS AND AMULETS

You've probably heard of talismans and amulets, but you may not know the difference between them. Many people confuse the two or lump them together under the catch-all term *charms*. Simply put, a talisman is designed to attract something or someone you desire. An amulet is intended to ward off something or someone you don't want in your life. Both can be fashioned for you or someone else.

People have been making and using talismans and amulets since antiquity. Gemstones, for example, have long been favored to either attract or repel. Ancient Greek soldiers carried bloodstone amulets into battle for protection. Aztec priests used gemstones to invoke the deities and for prophesying. Plants, images, and meaningful objects can all serve as talismans or amulets, as can special words and movements. Their magick resides not only in their essence, but also in the power you give them.

Egyptian Amulets

Amulets were popular among the ancient Egyptians, who often placed them in tombs to safeguard the souls of the deceased. According to D.J. Conway in *The Big Little Book of Magick*, "An ancient document known as the MacGregor Papyrus listed seventy-five different amulets, the names by which they were known, and their uses. This information is verified by a list carved on the walls of the temple at Dendera."

BOTANICAL LOVE TALISMAN

This talisman taps the energies of the plant kingdom to help you attract the right person into your life. Numbers play a role in the magick too. Two is the number of partnership and six symbolizes give-and-take. Perform this spell during the waxing moon, preferably when the moon is in Taurus or Libra, or on a Friday.

Tools and Ingredients

A circle of red silk cloth, 6" in
diameter
2 red rose petals
2 raspberry leaves
2 myrtle flowers

2 apple seeds
A piece of pink paper
A pen that writes red ink
A pink ribbon 6" long

1. Lay the circle of silk on your altar (or another surface).
2. Put the botanicals in the center of the silk circle while you contemplate what each one will do to enhance your spell.
3. On the piece of paper, write: "This talisman brings me a lover who is right for me in every way." Fold the paper three times, and then lay it on the botanicals.
4. Tie up the cloth to make a pouch containing the ingredients. Tie six knots in the ribbon, and repeat your intention aloud each time you tie a knot.
5. Carry the love talisman in your pocket or purse during the day and put it under your pillow at night until your wish comes true.

The Modern Witchcraft Book of Love Spells

WEAR A LOCKET TALISMAN

For centuries women have worn lockets as love talismans and keepsakes. You can enjoy this romantic tradition and strengthen your relationship at the same time. No one needs to know this pretty piece of jewelry is actually a magick spell. Wash the locket you purchase for this spell to remove any ambient vibrations before transforming it into a talisman.

Tools and Ingredients

A silver or gold locket
A small picture of your lover
A small picture of you
Clippings of your lover's hair
Clippings of your hair
Rose, jasmine, or ylang-ylang incense in a holder
Matches or a lighter

1. Open the locket and place the picture of your lover and the picture of you inside (or a photo of the two of you together).

2. Put some of your hair and some of your lover's hair in the locket and close it.

3. Light the incense, and then pass the locket through the smoke as you repeat this incantation (or one you compose yourself) three times:

"I love you and you love me,
We shall always joyful be."

4. Wear the locket to enhance your love and happiness; each time you touch it, you will be reminded of your intention.

A SAILOR'S VALENTINE

During the nineteenth century sailors created collages for their sweethearts using seashells to form intricate and beautiful designs; the designs often included a heart and were known as sailors' valentines. There's also an individual shell called a sailor's valentine that comes from the Pacific Ocean—it's shaped like a heart. You can purchase one from a shop that sells marine collectibles or online.

Tools and Ingredients

Essential oil of rose, jasmine, or ylang-ylang

A sailor's valentine

1. Dab some essential oil on the back of the shell; inhale the sensual fragrance of the oil as you hold your intention in your mind.
2. Carry the shell in your pocket or purse as a talisman to attract and/or enhance romance.

Create a Sailor's Valentine

If you're the crafty type, you may want to try your hand at creating a version of an antique valentine collage. Collect pretty shells, and then configure them in a design that you find pleasing. (You can find a lot of examples online if you need a little inspiration.) Give the valentine to your partner as a token of your love.

ATTRACT LOVE WITH A RUNE TALISMAN

The rune known as Gebo (or Gifu) is a letter from the Old Norse alphabet that looks like an X—the symbol we use to represent a kiss. Let this ancient glyph serve as a talisman to attract love.

Tools and Ingredients

A red or pink candle

Matches or a lighter

A piece of rose quartz, carnelian, garnet, jade, red jasper, or malachite
(cleansed)

Silver or gold nail polish

1. Set the candle on your altar or another place where you will craft this spell. Light the candle.

2. On the gemstone you've chosen, paint the X-shaped rune known as Gebo. As you work, consider what "love" means to you and what sort of relationship you intend to attract.

3. After the nail polish has dried, extinguish the candle.

4. Carry the gemstone with you as a talisman to attract love. Or, if you prefer, leave it on your altar or a windowsill in your bedroom.

PROTECT YOURSELF FROM UNWANTED ATTENTION

One of the most popular amulets among witches is the pentagram. This five-pointed star with a circle around it provides protection in all sorts of situations. Let it guard you against the attention of someone you don't want to bother you.

Tools and Ingredients

Pine essential oil

A silver or gold pentagram on a chain or black cord

1. Dab a little pine essential oil on the pentagram.

2. Wear the pentagram around your neck to serve as a shield against unwanted attention.

LOVE BRAID

To make this talisman, you weave together three things you seek in a relationship. You can do this spell to attract a new partner or to enhance aspects of an existing relationship. The symbolism of the number three brings your intention into the three-dimensional world.

Tools and Ingredients

3 ribbons, each 9" long (colors should correspond to your intentions: pink for affection, red for passion, green for abundance, blue for serenity, etc.)

A pen that writes silver or gold ink

1. On each ribbon, write one thing you desire in a relationship. As you write, focus on what you desire.

2. Tie the ribbons together at one end, and then braid the ribbons together. As you work, envision your desires manifesting.

3. When you've finished, tie a knot at the end of the braid and say aloud: "So mote it be."

4. Place the braid in your bedroom, or if you know feng shui, put it in the Relationship Gua of your home.

When Should You Make Talismans and Amulets?

Usually it's best to make talismans when the moon is waxing. Fashion talismans for love when the moon is in Taurus or Libra, the zodiac signs ruled by Venus, the planet of love and relationships. Amulets should be made when the moon is waning, preferably when the moon is in Capricorn, ruled by Saturn, the planet of limitation.

The Modern Witchcraft Book of Love Spells

SPIRIT ANIMAL TALISMAN

Do you have a spirit animal guide? Since ancient times people in many parts of the world have believed spirit animals lived in an invisible realm that intersects our own physical one. These spirit beings aided our ancestors in countless ways, from providing protection to offering healing wisdom to predicting the future. This spell petitions your spirit animal for help in attracting a lover.

Tools and Ingredients

A small stone figurine of the animal (jade, turquoise, red jasper, and malachite are good choices), cleansed
Incense (rose, ylang-ylang, jasmine, musk, or patchouli) in a burner
Matches or a lighter

1. Place the figurine on your altar.

2. Light the incense and ask the spirit animal, represented by the figurine, to help you attract a lover who's right for you in every way. As the smoke rises to the heavens, it carries your request to the spirit world.

3. When the incense has finished burning, pick up the figurine and carry it with you during the day. Place it on your nightstand while you sleep, where it will continue working its magick.

"Animals are sacred. They are living expressions of the divine principle—the Goddess and the God manifest in living form."
—TIMOTHY RODERICK, *THE ONCE UNKNOWN FAMILIAR*

TALISMAN TO IMPROVE COMMUNICATION

Men and women often have problems communicating because we think and process our emotions in different ways. Any relationship, however, can suffer from poor communication. This spell draws upon the power of the planet Mercury, which rules communication, to help you express yourselves better and promote better understanding between you.

Tools and Ingredients

A piece of pink paper

A pen or marker that writes
   blue ink

A white feather

An envelope

A book of love poems

1. On the piece of paper, write your desire to communicate better with your lover. If you have specific concerns or requests, you may state them, but in a positive way—don't gripe or accuse.

2. When you've finished, draw the symbol for Mercury on the paper. Close your eyes and imagine Mercury lending its energy to your spell.

3. Open your eyes and fold the paper three times, and then slip it into the envelope.

4. Put the feather in the envelope. Feathers symbolize the air element, the element that corresponds to communication.

5. Seal the envelope and slip it between the pages of the poetry book.

AMULET TO DEFLECT BAD FEELINGS

After a breakup people you know may side with your former partner and harbor bad feelings toward you. If their feelings are interfering with your well-being, this amulet can help deflect unpleasant energies away from you. Perform this spell during a waning moon.

Tools and Ingredients

2 pieces of citrine

Sage incense stick

Matches or a lighter

A mirror

1. Place the citrine (gold-colored quartz, known for its purifying properties) on your altar or carry it with you as you perform this spell.

2. Light the incense. Walk through your home carrying the incense and let its smoke purify everyplace you go.

3. When the sage finishes burning and you feel you've chased away all unwanted energies, pick up the mirror and go to the easternmost part of your home. Hold the mirror so the reflective side aims outward, to bounce back any negative energies that may be directed toward you.

4. Walk in a counterclockwise circle, holding the mirror out like a shield before you, as you say aloud:

> *"Whatever you say or do to me*
> *Returns to you multiplied by three."*

5. When you've completed a circuit and come back to the east again, drop to your knees and place your palms on the floor. Say aloud:

> *"Thoughts, words, and deeds cannot hurt me*
> *From your harm I'm forever free."*

6. Carry the piece of citrine with you as an amulet to negate any unwanted energies directed toward you and to protect you wherever you go.

"The value of love is the sum of what you have to pay for it and any time you get it cheap you have cheated yourself."
—WILLIAM FAULKNER, THE WILD PALMS

ASK A GODDESS TO IMPROVE YOUR RELATIONSHIP

Few relationships are perfect, and most hit snags occasionally. With this spell you call upon one of the goddesses of love—Venus, Aphrodite, Freya, or Hathor, for example—for assistance, as people have done for thousands of years. Whatever your problem, she can help.

Tools and Ingredients

3 runes: Gebo (Gifu), Wunjo, and Kenaz

A pink rose in a vase

Incense (rose, jasmine, ylang-ylang, or gardenia) in a holder

Matches or a lighter

A pink or red pouch, preferably silk

1. Select the runes from a set you don't use to do readings. Or, paint these symbols on small round stones. These runes represent love, joy, and passion respectively.

2. On your altar, arrange the runes in a triangle pattern. Triangles stimulate action.

3. Set the rose in its vase on your altar as a gift to the goddess you're petitioning.

4. Place the incense in the center of the triangle of runes, and light the incense.

5. As you watch the incense smoke, ask the deity to assist you in making your relationship better. When you sense her agreement, thank her.

6. Leave the runes and rose in place until the flower starts to wilt.

7. Remove the rose petals and allow them to dry. Place the dried petals and the runes in the pouch, and leave it on your altar to continue enhancing your relationship.

AMULET TO PROTECT YOUR HOME

This amulet protects your home from the unwanted intrusion of someone you'd rather not have contact with—an old lover or an unwanted suitor, for example. You can also use it to safeguard you from nonphysical beings who don't have your best interests at heart. Be sure to cleanse all the stones before you begin the spell.

Tools and Ingredients

Pine essential oil

A piece of amber

A piece of onyx

A piece of turquoise

Dried basil leaves

Dried ash leaves

Fennel seeds

A black drawstring pouch, preferably silk or leather

1. Dab a little pine essential oil on the gemstones. Add the stones and the botanicals to the pouch.

2. Tie the pouch shut while you say this incantation (or one you compose yourself) aloud:

> *"From energies I don't invite*
> *This spell protects me day and night."*

3. Hang the pouch on the inside of the exterior door of your home to provide protection. Envision yourself safe and sound, completely surrounded by a sphere of pure white light that no one can penetrate without your permission.

POWER BALANCING TALISMAN

In many relationships one person has more power than the other. This talisman uses the Chinese yin-yang symbol, which combines feminine and masculine energies in equal parts, to establish a better balance of power between you and a partner.

Tools and Ingredients

A smooth, round gray stone (cleansed)

Black paint

White paint

A paintbrush

1. Paint the yin-yang symbol on the stone. As you work, contemplate the meaning of the symbol, how the balance of both yin (feminine) and yang (masculine) forces is essential for the universe to function. Notice how the black (yin) and white (yang) halves entwine to form a whole, and how each contains a spot of its complement. If you are the more dominant person in your relationship, feel yourself softening and relinquishing some power to your lover. If you are the less dominant person, feel yourself growing stronger, taking more control and responsibility in the relationship.

2. Allow the paint to dry, and then place the stone on your altar or, if you know feng shui, in the Relationship Gua of your home. Whenever you need to reinforce your intention to create an equitable partnership, touch the talisman.

TALISMAN TO ATTRACT A NEW LOVER

Before you perform this spell, take some time to think about the traits and qualities you seek in a partner. Then distill them down to the three you consider most important. Next, refer to the tables in Chapter 3 and Chapter 4 for information about which ingredients to use in making this love talisman. Perform this spell on the new moon.

Tools and Ingredients

3 gemstones that represent what you seek in a love relationship (for example, carnelian for passion, rose quartz for affection and romance, diamond for commitment), cleansed

A piece of pink paper

A pen or marker, preferably with black ink

A pink or red drawstring pouch (silk is best)

3 botanicals that represent what you seek in a love relationship (for example, jasmine for harmony, geranium for fertility, or myrtle for good luck)

A small silvery heart charm

A small golden star charm

A stick or cone of incense (rose, jasmine, ylang-ylang, patchouli, or musk) in a holder

Matches or a lighter

A bowl of salt water

1. Place the gemstones on your altar or a table where you will craft your spell.

2. On the piece of pink paper, write the three things you most desire in a romantic partner. If you like, adorn the piece of paper with symbols, designs, or other illustrations that convey your wishes. When you've finished, fold the paper three times and slip it into the pouch.

3. Put the gemstones into the pouch. Add the botanicals, the heart charm (for love), and the star charm (for hope and luck).

4. Light the incense and hold the pouch in the wafting smoke for a few moments to charge the talisman with the elements fire and air while you imagine attracting the person you seek as a partner.

5. Sprinkle the pouch with the salt water to charge the talisman with the elements water and earth while you imagine attracting the person you seek as a partner. Say aloud:

> *"By the power of the four elements*
> *By the magick of three times three*
> *I attract a lover right and true*
> *And call [him or her] here to be with me."*

6. Place the talisman on your bedside table, sleep with it under your pillow, or carry it with you to send out a welcoming message to the person who's right for you.

"Talismans are actually a form of portable altar that we carry with us."

—D.J. CONWAY, *THE BIG LITTLE BOOK OF MAGICK*

VENUS TALISMAN FOR LUCK IN LOVE

Astrology gives the planet Venus dominion over love and relationships. Venus, as you may know, is usually the first "star" you see in the sky at night, so to petition her for aid, you'll recite an old English nursery rhyme you may remember from childhood. Do this spell just after dark on a clear night, during the moon's waxing phase.

The Modern Witchcraft Book of Love Spells

Tools and Ingredients

A piece of pink paper

A pen or marker that writes red ink

Essential oil of rose, jasmine, ylang-ylang, gardenia, patchouli, or musk

1. On the paper, draw two hearts interlocking. Write your name in one heart and your beloved's name in the other. If you don't currently have a lover but are seeking one, just write "my lover" in the second heart.

2. Next, draw the symbol for Venus above the two hearts. It looks like a circle with a cross below it—you may know it as the symbol for a woman.

3. Below the hearts, draw the symbol for what astrologers call the Part of Fortune. It looks like a circle with an X inside, touching the circle, and represents good luck. Envision your wishes manifesting happily.

4. When you've finished, dab a drop of essential oil on each corner of the paper, and then fold it three times. Hold the paper to your nose and inhale the scent, and then kiss the paper.

5. Go outside, taking the paper with you. Find Venus shining bright in the sky and hold the paper up toward her as you say aloud:

> *"Star light, star bright*
> *First star I see tonight*
> *I wish I may, I wish I might*
> *Have this wish I wish tonight."*

6. Carry the paper with you to continue attracting Venus's blessings and good luck in love.

Planets of the Gods and Goddesses

The ancients believed deities actually inhabited the planets in our solar system. According to this concept, the goddess Venus lives on the planet that bears her name.

AMULET TO BIND A FLIRTATIOUS FRIEND

Is a friend getting a little too friendly with your lover? Regardless of what your friend's intentions may be, it's time to put a stop to this flirtatious behavior.

Tools and Ingredients

A bunch of raffia

Black string

Tape

A photo of your friend

A black pouch

1. Form the raffia into a human-like shape, tying the string to fashion legs, arms, and a head. This symbolic form is known as a poppet.

2. Tape the photo of your friend on the poppet as you say aloud: "Creature of raffia, I name you [friend's name]."

3. Tie the poppet's hands together as you say aloud: "I now bind you and command you to keep your hands off [your lover's name]."

4. Put the poppet in the pouch and tie three knots to close it. Say aloud: "This is done for the good of all, harming none."

5. Place the poppet in the Friendship Gua of your home. To locate this spot, stand at the door you use most often to enter and leave your home, facing in. The Friendship Gua is to your far right.

"Whatever shape one creates must also create a deep emotional attraction or response. This principle is the core of sympathetic magick. For example, when shaping a candle so it bears the form of a pregnant woman in order to help with fertility, you must have tremendous love for this image of self and for the child growing in its belly, even though it's only a symbolic representation. In magick a symbol is just as potent as what it represents."

—Patricia Telesco, *Exploring Candle Magick*

Chapter 6

VISUAL SPELLS

In Chapter 1 we discussed the power of images in spellwork. Pictures, as you know, speak directly to your subconscious and the creative part of your brain. Before you can manifest something in the material world, you must first be able to imagine it, just as an architect must first envision a building before that building can take physical form.

The Law of Attraction, which Esther and Jerry Hicks popularized in their best-selling books, says that whatever you put your mind on you attract. That's why many of the spells in this book recommend visualizing what you desire and focusing your attention on that image while you perform the spell. In magick what you see really is what you get. In this chapter you'll learn how to work with pictures, colors, symbols, tarot cards, and other visuals to craft and cast love spells.

"The secret of achievement is to hold a picture of a successful outcome in mind."

—Henry David Thoreau

THE MAGICK OF COLORS

Colors influence us psychologically, emotionally, and physically, whether or not we realize it. Studies have shown that people tend to experience warm colors as stimulating, cool colors as as calming. Because we associate red with passion and pink with romance and affection, these are the colors witches use most often in doing love spells. However, other colors hold meanings too:

- Orange: enthusiasm, confidence, warmth
- Yellow: happiness, creativity, optimism
- Green: abundance, health, growth
- Blue: peace, clarity, cleansing
- Indigo: intuition, serenity
- Purple: wisdom, spirituality
- White: purity, protection
- Black: banishing negativity, boundaries, protection, power

You can bring color symbolism into your spells with candles, talisman and amulet pouches, gemstones, ribbons, clothing, flowers, and even food.

Elemental Colors

Magick workers connect the four elements—fire, water, air, and earth—with colors. Red corresponds to the fire element, blue to water, yellow to air, and green to earth.

SYMBOLS

Our world is replete with symbols. From the beginning of time, human beings have used symbols to convey ideas. Dream researchers examine the symbols that show up in our dreams to understand what the subconscious is trying to communicate. Numbers and geometric shapes are common symbols you see around you every day, usually without giving them a second thought. The average person recognizes only the obvious meanings of these familiar images, but to someone versed in occult knowledge they reveal something deeper. Astrological glyphs, the *I Ching*'s hexagrams, rune marks, alchemical symbols, and the suits on tarot cards are other examples of symbols that wise men and women have used for centuries.

In spellwork, you can tap the hidden meanings and your associations with symbols to get the results you desire. The heart, of course, is the most common symbol we connect with love, but here are some other popular symbols you may choose to use:

- Circle: wholeness, union, containment, protection
- Circle with a slash through it: rejection or banishing
- Square: stability, permanence
- Triangle pointing down: feminine energy
- Triangle pointing up: masculine energy
- Star: hope, good luck
- Rainbow: happiness, hope, blessings
- Cross: intersection of male and female, heaven and earth, spirit and matter
- Spiral: life energy

Also consider animal imagery. Bluebirds, for example, are linked with happiness. You probably have some personal symbols that hold special meaning for you, and those can be the most powerful of all.

MAGICK NUMBERS

Numbers are among the most common symbols in our lives. They're not only tools for keeping score; they also possess secret meanings that make them valuable in working magick. For example, we connect the number two with partnership, therefore many of the love spells in this book call for using two candles, two crystals, etc. Each number has distinct meanings you can tap in your spellwork:

- 1: beginnings, individuality, focus
- 2: partnership, balance, duality
- 3: creativity, expansion, good fortune
- 4: stability, structure
- 5: change, movement
- 6: harmony, cooperation, give-and-take
- 7: spirituality, retreat, self-reflection
- 8: permanence, boundaries, material mastery
- 9: transition, fulfillment, spiritual power

Numbers and the Tarot

The cards in the beautiful oracle known as the tarot feature numbers as well as other images and symbols. The numbers hold meanings that enable the person reading the cards to interpret them.

CREATE A SIGIL

A sigil is a uniquely personal symbol you design to produce a desired result. In a sense a sigil is a way of communicating with yourself via secret code, because no one else can interpret the symbol. Although there are various techniques for creating sigils, this one involves fashioning an image from letters.

Tools and Ingredients

A piece of paper

A pen or marker

1. On the piece of paper, write a word that states your intention: love, romance, passion, fidelity, commitment, or whatever your objective is for this spell. Delete any repeated letters; for example, "commitment" includes three *m*'s and two *t*'s, but you only need to put one of each into your design.

2. Entwine the remaining letters to form an image. You can use uppercase and/or lowercase letters, block or script. Position them right-side up, upside down, forward, or backward.

3. If you like, add other imagery that relates to your intention.

4. The end result depicts your objective in a graphic manner that your subconscious understands, although it won't make sense to anyone else.

5. Position your sigil on your altar, nightstand, or in a place where you'll see it often. Each time you look at the sigil, you'll instantly recognize its meaning at a deep level and that reinforces your intention.

You can add sigils to other spells—put them in talismans, carve them on candles, use them in formulating magick potions. For your own info, see the spell "A Drink for Lovers" in this chapter. I often incorporate them into my artwork. They're fun to design, and you'll probably use them a lot. In my book *The Modern Witchcraft Grimoire* you'll find a technique for creating sigils on another symbol known as a magick square.

"Reshape the images in your head to match the vision in your heart."

—Unknown

ROSE SPELL TO MAKE LOVE BLOSSOM

The well-known symbolic connection between roses and love helps to give this spell its power. Have fun making this pretty valentine and share it with your partner.

Tools and Ingredients

Red or pink construction paper

Scissors

A photo of you and your partner

Glue or tape

Pictures of roses from magazines

Rose petals

Optional: other pictures, lace, ribbon, glitter, etc.

Rose essential oil

1. From a sheet of construction paper cut a heart shape.
2. In the center of the paper heart glue or tape the photo of yourself and your partner.
3. Around the photo attach the pictures of roses and the rose petals. You may want to add other pictures, lace, ribbon, glitter, etc.
4. When you've finished, dab the heart with rose essential oil.
5. Give the valentine to your partner or display it where you'll see it often.

If you like, you can affix the heart to a larger piece of paper, fold the paper in half to make a card, and write a love note inside.

A DRINK FOR LOVERS

The rich imagery on tarot cards makes them ideal for spellworking. In fact, the tarot and magick are entwined—you'll notice many symbols common to witchcraft on the cards (for more on this, see my book *The Modern Witchcraft Book of Tarot*).

Tools and Ingredients

2 pink or red candles in holders

Matches or a lighter

The Two of Cups from a tarot deck (ideally, the card should picture two people toasting with chalices)

Wine, apple cider, or spring water

A chalice or wineglass

1. Set the candles on your altar (or another surface where they can burn safely) and light them.

2. Lay the tarot card face-up between the candles.

3. Pour the wine, apple cider, or spring water into the chalice or wineglass, and then set it on the tarot card. The images on the card will imprint the beverage with meaning.

4. Leave the chalice or wineglass in place for six minutes, while you hold loving thoughts in your mind, and then drink the beverage. You may want to share the drink with your partner.

5. Allow the candles to burn down completely. Leave the card in place overnight.

"The heart is
The thousand-stringed instrument
That can only be tuned with Love."

—HAFIZ, *THE GIFT*

YOUR EMBLEM OF LOVE

In this spell you combine several symbols to design a personal love emblem. An emblem is a symbolic device that serves as an identifying sign or mark, like a family crest.

Tools and Ingredients

A 6" square of red or pink cloth

Pens or markers that write on cloth

1. On the cloth draw a circle 3" in diameter.
2. Inside the circle, draw two intersecting triangles, one pointing up and the other pointing down to represent the union of masculine and feminine forces. (It will look like a Star of David.)
3. In the center of the intersecting triangles draw a small heart.
4. Around the outside of the circle draw a lot of little five-pointed stars.
5. At each corner of the cloth draw a sigil that expresses something you want in your relationship.
6. If you wish, you can add other symbols that hold meaning for you. When you've finished, display your emblem where you'll see it often.

LOVERS' HEART

You've probably seen hearts with initials in them carved into tree trunks as testaments to two people's love. However, cutting into a tree is harmful—the bark is the tree's skin. This spell uses the same imagery but doesn't hurt a tree.

Tools and Ingredients

A heart-shaped leaf   Rosewater (see Chapter 4)

A Sharpie or other marker

1. Write your initials and your lover's on the leaf.

2. Lay the leaf at the base of a tree. It may be one of the trees dubbed sacred by the ancient Celts (see Chapter 4) or one with which you feel an affinity.

3. Ask the tree to help your love grow strong. Pour some rosewater on the ground as a thank-you gift to the tree for its assistance.

LIGHT MY FIRE

The symbolism in this spell is obvious. Perform it to spark passion in the heart of someone new or fan the flames in an existing relationship.

Tools and Ingredients
A red candle
A ballpoint pen, nail, athame, or other pointed tool
Candle-Dressing Lotion (see Chapter 7)
A candleholder
A ring large enough to slide over the candle
Matches or a lighter

1. On the candle carve your name and your partner's with your pointed tool so that the letters are alternated and interspersed. For example, Bill and Sue would be written: B S I U L E L.

2. Anoint the candle with the lotion and fit the candle into the holder. Set it on your altar or another surface where it can burn safely over a period of several days.

3. Slide the ring onto the candle and light the candle. As you stare into the flame, chant the word created by your joint names. Envision a union between you and your partner.

4. When you can no longer concentrate on the spell, snuff out the candle.

5. Repeat each day until the candle has burned down to the ring. Remove the ring and place it under your mattress to "fire up" a romance.

WITCH'S LADDER

The term *witch's ladder* refers to a series of knots into which you tie your intentions. You need only minimal sewing skills to craft and cast this spell.

Tools and Ingredients

A cloth handkerchief (white, or a color that suits your intentions)
A needle and thread (white, or a color that suits your intentions)
Scissors

1. After forming your intention in your mind, begin sewing a witch's ladder into the handkerchief. Start at the top left corner and make a single stitch, and then a knot.

2. As you tie the knot, say aloud an affirmation or incantation that states your intention.

3. Repeat until you've sewn a line of stitches and knots from the top left corner to the bottom right corner.

4. Start again at the top right corner, and repeat until you've sewn a line of stitches and knots to the bottom left corner, forming an X across the handkerchief.

5. Depending on your intention, you may choose to give the handkerchief to your lover, carry it with you, or put it under your pillow while you sleep.

Cross-Stitch Magick

Cross-stich is one of the oldest forms of needlework, dating back to the sixth century B.C.E. It uses a series of Xs to create a design. Because we associate the X with a kiss and love, you can use cross-stitch embroidery to create a design that's a magickal work of art.

CULTIVATE AN ATTITUDE OF GRATITUDE

Wiccans subscribe to the belief that whatever you send out (in thought, word, or deed) will return to you. Therefore, it stands to reason that cultivating an attitude of gratitude would attract more blessings. In this spell you visually express thanks for the good things in your life.

Tools and Ingredients

One or more designated pages in your grimoire or journal

Pictures of things for which you're thankful

Glue or tape

Colored pens, pencils, or markers

1. Designate a section in your grimoire or journal for expressing gratitude. You may choose to do this once or on a daily basis—or at any time you choose.

2. Collect photographs of you, your lover, and things that are part of your relationship for which you are grateful (such as your children, home, pets, etc.). Also consider including pictures from magazines that stimulate loving feelings in you, images downloaded from online sources, etc.

3. Glue or tape the pictures into your grimoire or journal. Beside them, write expressions of gratitude for whatever these pictures express and symbolize.

4. Add other loving images, words, etc. that relate to the pictures you've chosen to include in your grimoire or journal. Devote as many pages as you need to express what you want to express. Each loving thought attracts more love to you.

5. Flip through your grimoire or journal often to review the many blessings in your life and to give thanks. Continue adding more images and comments whenever you wish.

THE GAME OF LOVE

In the fifteenth century the Spanish nobility played a game called *juego de naipes* with forty-nine cards. These cards were used to tell fortunes and reveal secrets, particularly regarding matters of the heart. Each card had a verse written on it, composed of the same number of lines as the card's number. Take your cue from this colorful game to cast a love spell using a tarot card.

Tools and Ingredients

A tarot deck you don't use for readings

A pen or marker

1. Choose a card that represents your intention. If you aren't familiar with the meanings of the cards, you can look them up online or read about them in my book *The Modern Witchcraft Book of Tarot*.

2. What's the number on the card? That number determines the number of statements you'll make related to your intention. If, for example, you've selected a card numbered 6 you'll create six affirmations that describe your objective.

3. On the back of the card, write the statements you've designed to produce the outcome you desire. These statements can be as simple or eloquent as you wish, but they should all relate to a single intention—for example, to attract a new lover or resolve a problem in a current relationship.

4. When you've finished, you may choose to display the card on your altar or another place where you'll see it often. Or, slip the card in an envelope and put it under your pillow at night. Depending on your intention, you might want to give the card to your lover.

I CHING SPELL TO UNITE WITH A PARTNER

Believed to have been created by Confucius, the ancient Chinese oracle known as the *I Ching* is composed of twenty-six patterns called hexagrams. Each design contains six lines, configured in different ways, and each has a special meaning.

Tools and Ingredients

A pink or red candle

A ballpoint pen, nail, athame, or other pointed tool

A candleholder

Matches or a lighter

1. On the candle, inscribe the image "Pi" (Holding Together) with your pointed tool.

2. Fit the candle into the candleholder and light it. As the candle burns, the energy inherent in the image is released into the universe to bring you and a partner together.

"A stray fact: insects are not drawn to candle flames, they are drawn to the light on the far side of the flame, they go into the flame and sizzle to nothingness because they're so eager to get to the light on the other side."

—MICHAEL CUNNINGHAM, *BY NIGHTFALL*

THE COLOR OF LOVE

Recently, adults have rediscovered how much fun it is to color, and sales of coloring books for adults have skyrocketed. Because spellwork requires creativity and visual ability, you can tap your innate talents in this colorful manner to work magick. Choose an image that represents love to you for this spell. You can take one from a coloring book or download one from the Internet.

Tools and Ingredients
A red or pink candle in a holder

Matches or a lighter

A black-and-white image of hearts and flowers

Crayons, markers, or color pencils

1. Set the candle on a table or other surface where you will give your creative talents free rein, and light the candle.

2. Color the image you've chosen according to your intentions and preferences. You may want to emphasize colors associated with love, such as red, pink, and purple. However, there's no right or wrong way to express your creativity.

3. While you work, keep your attention focused on your intention. Each mark you make should be designed to enhance your objective. Coloring helps to relax you and focuses your thoughts in a gentle way. The more energy you can bring to the process, the more effective your magick will be.

4. When you're finished, display your artwork in a place where you'll see it often.

SPELL TO REPEL UNWANTED ADVANCES

If your goal is to block the unwanted advances of someone, use the witch's pentagram as a protection aid. Although in this spell the final image is invisible, the energy you invest in your visualization during the process provides the spell's power. Perform this spell during the waning moon, preferably when the moon is in Capricorn.

Tools and Ingredients

A saucepan

Water

8 fresh basil leaves

Fennel seeds

A sprig of rosemary

8 white carnation petals

A wooden spoon

A sieve or colander

A small paintbrush

1. In a saucepan, heat water until it almost boils.

2. Add the botanicals, and then reduce heat to simmer. Stir three times in a counterclockwise direction to charge the mix.

3. Brew for eight minutes, and then strain out the botanicals and set them aside. Save the liquid.

4. When the brew has cooled, carry the saucepan to your front door. Dip the paintbrush in the liquid and paint a pentagram on the exterior of your door. As you work, visualize you and your home being protected by the magickal pentagram.

5. Repeat at each door of your home that leads to the outside. If you wish, paint pentagrams on the windowsills too.

6. Take whatever herbal water remains and pour it on the ground outside your front door (or the door you use most often to enter and exit your home).

7. Allow the protection herbs to dry, and then scatter them in front of your home to prevent unwanted advances from people with whom you don't want to have contact.

WRITE A SPELL WITH OGHAM RUNES

Throughout the British Isles and Ireland you can see stones on which messages have been engraved in Ogham runes. As discussed in Chapter 4, the letters in this early Celtic alphabet are based on trees. You can find a table of the Ogham letters in my book *The Modern Witchcraft Grimoire* or online, and use these runes in spellwork.

Tools and Ingredients

A smooth round stone (cleansed)

A marker, paint, or nail polish

1. Compose in your mind a short affirmation that expresses your intention.

2. Write your affirmation on the stone using Ogham runes. Draw the individual letters so they are connected to one another, forming a continuous line in a circle around the stone. Hold your intention in your mind as you work.

3. Set the stone on your altar or in another place where you will see it often. If the stone is small enough, you can carry it with you.

FENG SHUI SPELL FOR A HAPPY RELATIONSHIP

The ancient Chinese art of placement known as feng shui (pronounced "fung sway") offers many practical advantages, but it's also a form of magick. According to this system, each area (or gua) of your home corresponds to an area of your life. Although a number of different feng shui schools of thought exist, the one I practice says that when you stand at the door you use most often to enter and exit your home, the far right-hand sector represents your primary partnership. Everything in that sector affects your relationship, and by changing something in this gua you can change the relationship itself.

Tools and Ingredients

Incense or a sage wand

Matches or a lighter

A picture of a happy couple, such as Renoir's *Dance at Bougival*

1. Clear away clutter from the Relationship Gua of your home. Cleanse the area of dirt and smudge it to get rid of unwanted energies. Remove anything that doesn't remind you of love and happiness.

2. Hang the picture you've chosen in this gua. The joy depicted in the picture will activate positive energy in your primary relationship.

3. Enter this section of your home every day to keep the energy there activated.

SPELL TO END A RELATIONSHIP PEACEFULLY

Ending a romantic relationship is often painful, although you can use magick to help bring closure in a peaceful way. This spell draws upon the familiar imagery of a circle with a slash through it that we associate with "no."

Tools and Ingredients

A photo of you and your former partner
A piece of white paper
Tape or glue
A pen or marker that writes black ink
White poppy petals
A cauldron or flameproof pot
Matches or a lighter

1. Attach a photo of you and your former partner to a piece of white paper with tape or glue.
2. Draw a circle with a slash through it on the photo. Around the photo draw images that represent peace to you: doves, olive branches, peace signs, etc. Write words or affirmations, such as "Let there be peace between us always and in all ways" or something more poetic or personal.
3. Lay the poppy petals on the photo, and then fold the paper three times.
4. Hold the paper and photo slightly above the cauldron and light the paper—be careful not to burn yourself. Drop the paper into the cauldron and watch it burn while you send peaceful thoughts into the flame. Your thoughts will be released into the universe.
5. Scatter the cooled ashes in a peaceful place away from your home.

The Modern Witchcraft Book of Love Spells

Chapter 7

LOVE POTIONS AND LOTIONS

Remember the witches' brew in Shakespeare's *Macbeth*? In his famous play, the bard's characters concocted a magick potion this way:

> *"Fillet of a fenny snake,*
> *In the cauldron boil and bake;*
> *Eye of newt, and toe of frog,*
> *Wool of bat, and tongue of dog,*
> *Adder's fork, and blind-worm's sting,*
> *Lizard's leg, and owlet's wing,*
> *For a charm of powerful trouble,*
> *Like a hell-broth boil and bubble."*

The magick potions and lotions in this chapter draw upon the energies of botanicals, crystals and gemstones, affirmations and incantations, and most importantly, your personal power.

Tasting Magick Brews
Although it's unlikely you'll ever encounter a brew as vile as the one described in Shakespeare's play, many magickal concoctions don't taste very good. Sometimes you can improve their flavor with a little honey, but remember, their purpose isn't to delight the palate.

MAGICK MASSAGE OIL

Use this fragrant massage oil to enhance love and sensuality between you and a partner. Choose a single essential oil, or combine two or more to make a blend you like and that suits your intentions. Dab a little of the mixture on your skin as a test.

Tools and Ingredients

4 ounces olive, grapeseed, or jojoba oil

A clear glass jar or bottle with a lid

Several drops essential oil (rose, jasmine, ylang-ylang, patchouli, vanilla, or musk)

A piece of pink paper

Colored pens, pencils, or markers

Scissors

Tape

1. Pour the carrier oil into the bottle.

2. Add essential oil a little at a time until the scent is as strong as you want it to be. Shake the bottle three times to combine the oils and charge the mixture.

3. On the paper, draw images that represent love to you. You may also want to write an affirmation on the paper, stating your intention.

4. Cut the paper to make a label and tape it to the bottle, with the images facing in. They will infuse the oil with your intention.

5. Store the oil in a cool, dark place between massages.

HARMONY POTION

Seven is a mystical and magickal number that signifies wholeness—there are seven colors in the visible spectrum, seven major chakras in the human body, and seven tones in a musical scale. This potion uses sound to encourage harmony in your relationship.

Tools and Ingredients

7 ounces spring water

A clear glass bottle

The 7 notes of a musical scale

1. Pour the spring water into the bottle.

2. Play the seven notes on a CD, a musical instrument, singing bowls, tuning forks, etc. The resonances will be absorbed into the water and charge it.

3. Drink the water to incorporate the harmonious resonances into your energy field. As you drink, feel yourself becoming peaceful and balanced. Envision this feeling expanding into your relationship, making it more harmonious and joyful. You may want to share the charged water with your lover.

4. If you like, you can also put a drop or two of the water on each of your major chakras.

TEA FOR TWO

Share this aromatic herbal tea with a partner to celebrate your love. It offers health benefits as well as magickal ones.

Tools and Ingredients

1 cup dried rose hips

A blender or food processor

⅛ cup dried grated orange rind

¼ cup dried peppermint leaves

A glass jar with a lid

A teapot

Boiling water

Honey to taste

1. Put the rose hips in the blender or food processor and grind them.

2. Put the ground rose hips in the jar, and then add the orange rind and peppermint leaves. Combine.

3. When you're ready to brew this drink, put one teaspoon of the botanical mix in the teapot for each cup of tea you're making, plus one teaspoon "for the pot."

4. Boil water and add it to the teapot. Let the tea steep for several minutes until it's as strong as you want it to be. Serve with honey.

5. Store the tea in a cool, dark place—sunlight will cause it to deteriorate.

SENSUALITY TEA

Delicate jasmine flowers don't just add a pleasant fragrance and flavor to food; they can also enhance sensuality and encourage romantic feelings. Enjoy this exotic tea with your lover.

Tools and Ingredients

3 cups spring water (you can use more or less, depending on how strong you want the brew)

A saucepan

2 tablespoons dried jasmine flowers (if you can't find the flowers, you can use packaged jasmine tea)

½ teaspoon grated fresh ginger

A fine-mesh sieve

2 teacups

1. Put the water in the saucepan along with the jasmine flowers and ginger. Heat, and allow the brew to simmer about five minutes.

2. Strain the tea to remove the botanicals, and then pour it into the teacups. Sip the tea while you focus on your love.

TRUTH SERUM

Do you suspect your lover isn't telling you the truth? This spell lets you connect psychically with your partner to see through the smokescreen and get to the heart of the matter. Drink this magick tea to open your second sight—but be sure you're ready to know the truth.

Tools and Ingredients

2 cups spring water

A pot or kettle

¼ cup fresh nettle leaves

1 teaspoon dried chamomile flowers

3 large yarrow leaves

A teacup

Honey to taste

A dark blue candle in a holder

Matches or a lighter

1. Pour the water into the pot or kettle and boil.

2. Reduce heat, add the botanicals, and simmer about six minutes.

3. Strain out the botanicals and pour the tea into the cup. Add honey.

4. Set the candle on your altar or other surface and light the candle.

5. Sip the tea slowly while you allow your mind to relax and grow receptive. Think of your lover and the issue about which you have concerns.

6. When you feel ready to learn the truth, look into the candle's flame. Pay attention, for the answer may come in one of a number of ways: You might see visions, feel a reaction in your body, or merely sense what's true. Trust your intuition.

HONEY LOTION

Hedge and kitchen witches are magick workers who practice an uncomplicated style of spellcraft that values the blessings of everyday life, including food, home, and hearth. This love lotion draws upon the qualities of two amazing foods to work its magick: the sweet nature of honey and the purifying properties of coconut oil.

Tools and Ingredients

4 ounces coconut oil

1 ounce honey

A small saucepan

A wooden spoon

Pink or red rose petals, finely snipped

A plain glass jar with a lid

1. Put the coconut oil and honey in the saucepan; heat until liquid, stirring in a clockwise direction.

2. Let it cool to a comfortably warm temperature, and then add the rose petals, working them into the mixture with your hands.

3. Use as a sensuous massage lotion. Store the remaining lotion in a glass jar. In cool weather the lotion will solidify, but you can warm it up again prior to use.

Honey's Eternal Magick

Not only is honey delicious and healthy; it also lasts practically forever. Archaeologists have discovered honey in ancient Egyptian tombs—and it's still unspoiled, even after thousands of years. If you're doing a spell to make love last, add a bit of honey to the brew.

CRYSTAL ELIXIR

Make this magick elixir on the night of the full moon to maximize its benefit. This version calls for a clear quartz crystal, but you can experiment with various crystals and gemstones according to your purposes (see Chapter 3 for more information).

Tools and Ingredients

A clear quartz crystal (cleansed)

6 ounces spring water

A glass jar with a lid (cleansed)

1. Hold the crystal to your "third eye" (on your forehead, between your eyebrows). Keep your intention in your mind and project it into the crystal.
2. Pour the water into the jar. Add the crystal and shake the jar gently three times to charge the water.
3. Leave the jar on a windowsill where the moon can shine on it overnight.
4. In the morning, remove the crystal and drink the elixir.

Reading Tea Leaves

Tasseography is the art of interpreting meaning from patterns formed by the residue of tea leaves in a cup. This divination practice gained popularity in Europe during the seventeenth century, after tea was introduced from China by Dutch traders. The term derives from the French word *tasse*, meaning "cup."

CANDLE-DRESSING LOTION

Candles, as you know, play an important role in many magick spells and rituals. To enhance or fine-tune their power, witches often anoint candles with specially formulated oils or other substances, a practice known as "dressing" the candles. You can use this lotion in most love spells.

Tools and Ingredients

2 ounces almond oil

A dark green glass jar or bottle with a lid or stopper

3 apple seeds, finely ground

2 drops bergamot essential oil

A pink ribbon, 6" long

1. Pour the almond oil into the jar or bottle; add the apple seeds and essential oil. Shake three times to charge.

2. Tie the ribbon around the jar or bottle, making three knots. Store the oil in a cool, dark place.

How to Dress Candles

The way you apply oil to a candle can influence a spell. To attract something, pour a little oil in your palm. Start at the top of the candle and slowly rub the oil downward to the middle. Then, rub oil from the bottom of the candle up to the middle. To repel, release, or banish something, start at the middle of the candle and rub the oil to the bottom, and then from the middle to the top of the candle. (Note: Try not to get oil on the candle's wick.)

CHAKRA-ENHANCING WATER

According to Hindu belief, our bodies have seven major "chakras," or vortices through which energy circulates. These chakras are aligned roughly along the spine, from the tailbone to the top of the head. Each chakra corresponds to a color. This potion uses colors to harmonize the energy of your chakras.

Tools and Ingredients

Spring water

A clear glass

Food coloring

1. Pour the water into the glass.

2. Add two drops of food coloring to the water. Green corresponds to the heart chakra and encourages loving feelings. Orange relates to the sacral chakra (about a hand's width below your bellybutton), which is the seat of sexual energy. Light blue is linked with the throat chakra, the center associated with communication. (You can find more information about the chakras online.)

3. Swirl the food coloring in the water while you contemplate your intention.

4. Sip the water and feel it working its magick. You may also want to dot a little of the enhanced water on the related chakra to promote harmony.

"Love is like a magic potion that once drunk leads you into the alchemy of complete transformation."

—Manuela Dunn Mascetti, *Rumi: The Path of Love*

UNDINE EMOTION POTION

Undines (or ondines) are elemental beings that animate the element of water. Most people don't see them, but sometimes, if you look closely, you'll spot them swirling on the surface of a body of water. Although mythology often portrays them as mermaids, Nancy B. Watson in her book *Practical Solitary Magic* describes them as resembling jelly doughnuts. The element of water is linked with emotions and relationships; therefore the undines can assist you in matters of the heart. But there's a catch: You must give them a thank-you gift. That's where this potion comes in handy.

Tools and Ingredients

An empty wine bottle with a cap or cork

6 ounces spring water

2 ounces red wine

Essential oil (rose, ylang-ylang, jasmine, gardenia, or another that suits
    your purpose)

Dried pink or red rose petals, crumbled

1. Soak the label off the wine bottle.

2. Pour the spring water into the wine bottle, and then add the red wine and a few drops of essential oil.

3. Add the rose petals to the bottle and shake three times to charge the potion, and then cap or cork the bottle.

4. Take the potion with you to a body of water that you like—a pond, lake, stream, etc.—and sit near the water. As you gaze at the water, allow your mind to relax and your vision to soften—perhaps you'll notice swirls or flattish bubbles on the surface of the water. That often means the undines are there.

5. Ask the undines to help you with some facet of your love life. Sit quietly and try to sense a response from these elementals. Even if you don't see or sense them, they may still be present and willing to offer aid.

6. Thank the undines. Pour the potion into the water to show gratitude.

ADD SPARKLE TO YOUR LOVE LIFE

It's not uncommon for some of the sparkle in a relationship to fade over time. This glittery massage lotion helps rekindle the spark you enjoyed when you first fell in love.

Tools and Ingredients

3 ounces olive, almond, grapeseed, or jojoba oil

A glass jar with a lid

A few drops of cinnamon essential oil

Gold glitter

2 red candles in holders

Matches or a lighter

1. Pour the olive (or other) oil into the jar. Add the cinnamon essential oil and gold glitter. Shake three times to combine the ingredients and charge the lotion.

2. Set the candles in a safe place and light them.

3. Share a luxurious massage with your partner. Notice how the glitter sparkles in the candlelight!

Amortentia

Billed as the most powerful love potion of all—at least in the world of Harry Potter—Amortentia is unique in that it smells different to each person. That's because each of us finds different scents appealing. The potion's name derives from the Latin word for love: *amor.*

HAPPINESS POTION

Many love potions are designed to stimulate sexual desire, ensure fidelity, or deepen love. This one focuses on bringing happiness into any relationship—you can use it for friendship as well as for romance.

Tools and Ingredients

Sparkling apple cider	A pinch of marjoram
A chalice or wineglass	A daisy
A piece of tumbled jade	The Sun card from a tarot deck

1. Pour the apple cider into your chalice or a wineglass.
2. Add the jade, and then sprinkle in the marjoram and float the daisy blossom on top.
3. Lay the Sun tarot card face-up on your altar; set the chalice or wineglass on top of the card for ten minutes so it can absorb the joyful energy symbolized by the Sun card.
4. Remove the daisy and the jade, and then drink the joy-infused cider. When you've finished, eat the flower's petals. (Yes, you really can eat the daisies.)
5. Return the tarot card to its deck.

HOT CHOCOLATE LOVE POTION

What could be more pleasant on a cold day than drinking a cup of hot chocolate? But did you know that chocolate contains a chemical known as phenylethylamine that triggers the release of endorphins in your brain? These "feel-good" compounds mimic the sensation of being in love.

Tools and Ingredients

Hot chocolate

A pretty mug

Vanilla extract to taste

A cinnamon stick

Orange peel, finely grated

1. Pour the hot chocolate into a pretty mug—a pink or red one, or one decorated with images you associate with love.

2. Add a little vanilla extract and stir with the cinnamon stick, making three clockwise circles to charge the brew. Sprinkle the orange peel on top.

3. As you sip the drink, envision it increasing your ability to give and receive love. Sense your heart opening. Feel yourself becoming more loving in every way. Allow these feelings to expand into the universe, and (if it's your intention) to draw a lover to you. If you like, share this drink with a lover.

THIRTEEN-FLOWER POTION

We associate flowers with love, especially roses, but we don't often think about eating them. Each flower has a distinct flavor, as well as unique healing properties and magickal associations (see Chapter 4 for more info). Some can be used in salads, breads, and other dishes—for example, jasmine adds a delicate flavor to rice, and nasturtiums lend a pleasing zing to salads. To make this potion, however, all you need to do is add a bit of each flower (after washing them and removing their stems and leaves) to a blender along with apple juice.

Tools and Ingredients

Bee balm	Rose
Calendula	Squash blossom
Daisy	Sunflower
Echinacea	Violet
Honeysuckle	Apple juice (as much as you
Jasmine	want to use)
Lavender	A blender
Nasturtium	A glass (with no images on it)
Pansy	

1. Put all the flowers and the juice in a blender and combine until smooth.
2. Pour the mixture into the glass. Drink the floral potion while you envision it drawing love and blessings to you.

Note: You may not be able to acquire all these flowers fresh— it's okay to substitute some other types that are more readily available or that better suit your intentions. Do a little research first, though, to make sure the flowers you choose are edible—steer clear of wolfsbane, foxglove, and lily of the valley!

Lucky Number Thirteen

All sorts of negative and scary superstitions surround the number thirteen. Some people say it signifies the number of men at the Last Supper. It's also the number on the Death card of the tarot. For witches, however, it represents the number of lunar months in a year and therefore is a lucky number.

BANISHING LOTION

When you end a relationship or feel a need to put distance between yourself and someone else, use this lotion to create an energetic barrier. Coconut oil contains purifying properties; basil is a popular protection herb. Make this lotion during the waning moon, preferably on Saturday or when the moon is in Capricorn, to maximize its effectiveness.

Tools and Ingredients

4 ounces coconut oil

8 fresh basil leaves, finely snipped

A small saucepan

A wooden spoon

A plain glass jar with a lid

1. Put the coconut oil and basil leaves in the saucepan; heat at a medium-low temperature until the oil melts, stirring in a counterclockwise direction.

2. After the mixture has cooled to a comfortably warm temperature, dip your finger in the lotion and draw a pentagram on your chest, near your heart, as a symbol of protection. If you wish, draw pentagrams with the lotion on other parts of your body too—for example, on your lower back, or root chakra.

3. Store the remaining lotion in a glass jar. In cool weather the lotion will solidify, but you can warm it up again prior to use.

WITCH'S BREW

Once you've had some practice mixing magick potions, you can begin concocting your own original "witch's brews" for special purposes. Perform this spell with a lover. How trusting—and trustworthy—are you?

Tools and Ingredients

Depends on your intention and what you decide to put in your spell

1. With your partner, agree that each of you will formulate a potion for the other. Don't tell each other what's in your potions or what results these mysterious brews are likely to produce. Ideally, the potions should be designed to help the other person achieve his or her goals, overcome a problem, or attract a benefit.

2. Concoct your potions separately, in private.

3. Exchange potions and drink them together. Then wait and see what happens. Share your reactions with each other, and then record what you did in your grimoire.

Chapter 8

EDIBLE SPELLS

According to what's known as sympathetic magick, like attracts like. In spellwork, an item can serve as a representative or stand-in for another item that's similar to it in some way. Similarities are not coincidental and they signify a connection—physical, spiritual, energetic, or otherwise—between the two items.

Therefore, we eat sweet treats to increase the sweetness in our lives. Eggs symbolize fertility. Some correspondences are based on color; for example, red cherries make us think of love. Others are due to shapes; avocados and peaches, when pitted, bear a resemblance to the womb, whereas bananas and cucumbers are phallic in appearance.

FOODS TO USE IN LOVE SPELLS	
Fruit	Apples, apricots, bananas, cherries, mangos, red grapes, peaches, raspberries, strawberries
Vegetables	Avocados, beans, carrots, cucumbers, rhubarb, sweet potatoes, tomatoes
Grains	Rice, wheat
Seafood	Crabmeat, oysters, salmon, shrimp
Sweets	Chocolate, honey, maple syrup, sugar
Other	Eggs, nuts

BREAKFAST DELIGHTS

Pancakes with Maple Syrup

Use pure, natural maple syrup and real butter with these pancakes—artificial substitutes don't contain the same positive energy as the real deal.

YIELDS ABOUT 12 PANCAKES

Tools and Ingredients

A griddle

1½ cups all-purpose flour

2½ teaspoons baking powder

1½ tablespoons granulated sugar

½ teaspoon salt

A mixing bowl

A mixing spoon

A small bowl

1 egg, beaten

1 cup whole milk

3 tablespoons butter, melted

A pancake turner

Butter

Maple syrup

1. Warm the griddle while you combine the dry ingredients in the mixing bowl.
2. In the small bowl, stir together the beaten egg, milk, and butter using a clockwise motion (clockwise circles attract).
3. Add the liquid mixture to the flour mixture and stir using a clockwise motion. Mix only until ingredients are combined—don't beat or try to get the batter really smooth, or your pancakes won't be light and fluffy.
4. Pour batter onto the hot griddle, forming heart-shaped pancakes. When bubbles form on the top of the batter, flip the pancakes. They should be golden brown.
5. Stack the pancakes on plates and top with butter and maple syrup.
6. Optional: Serve with your favorite fresh fruit from the list given earlier in this chapter (such as sliced peaches, berries, or cooked apples).

Fruit Smoothies

Pick your favorite fruit to combine in quick-and-easy fruit smoothies. These magickal blends are perfect for breakfast or lunch, or when you're in a rush and don't want to turn to unhealthy fast food.

YIELDS 3–4 SERVINGS

Tools and Ingredients

A blender

2 cups fresh fruit (from the table given earlier in this chapter), washed and cut into bite-sized pieces

Plain Greek-style yogurt (amount depends on how thick you like your smoothie and what other ingredients you've chosen)

Fruit juice, herb tea, or water (amount depends on how thick you like your smoothie)

1. Put chopped fresh fruit in the blender.
2. Add yogurt and fruit juice (or other liquid), and blend until smooth.
3. As you drink this mix of goddess-blessed fruit, imagine love flowing to you from every direction, enriching your life in every way.

"A tree is known by its fruit; a man by his deeds. A good deed is never lost; he who sows courtesy reaps friendship, and he who plants kindness gathers love."

—SAINT BASIL

Raspberry Scones

Enjoy these fluffy, berry-rich scones for breakfast, at tea, or anytime you want to sweeten your love life. While you prepare them, remember to think loving thoughts to infuse the scones with magick.

YIELDS ABOUT 20

Tools and Ingredients

2½ cups all-purpose flour (you'll need a little more to sprinkle on your work surface to keep dough from sticking)

¼ cup granulated sugar

1 tablespoon baking powder

½ teaspoon salt

Food processor or mixer

1 stick butter (not softened), cut into small pieces

¾ cup buttermilk (you can substitute regular whole milk if you prefer)

1 egg yolk

A small bowl

A whisk or fork

6 ounces fresh raspberries

2 baking sheets, lined with parchment paper or greased

1. Preheat oven to 400°F.
2. Put all the dry ingredients into food processor or mixer and combine. Add the butter and mix until you have pea-sized bits.
3. Pour the milk and egg yolk into the bowl and whisk together, and then add slowly to the flour mixture. Mix just until the batter is combined—don't overwork the dough.
4. Spread dough on a lightly floured work surface and sprinkle berries on top.
5. Gently knead the berries into the dough, trying not to crush the berries—don't overwork the dough (if you handle it too much the scones won't be fluffy).

6. Pull off pieces of dough about 1" in diameter and place them on the baking sheets, about 2" apart.

7. Bake about 15 minutes, or until scones are lightly browned. Cool on wire racks before serving.

SEDUCTIVE SALADS

Strawberry Salad

The strawberries in this pretty salad remind you of love—especially when you share it with a partner. It won't keep, so you can half the recipe if you like. For a complete summer meal, add roasted chicken cut into bite-sized pieces.

YIELDS 4 SERVINGS

Tools and Ingredients
Juice of 1 large garlic bulb (or more to taste)
½ cup olive oil
1 tablespoon balsamic vinegar
A large salad bowl
A whisk
1 pint fresh strawberries, sliced, stems discarded
8 ounces mixed salad greens
½ cup pecans, whole or chopped
4 ounces goat cheese, crumbled

1. Pour the garlic juice, olive oil, and balsamic vinegar into the bowl; whisk together to blend.

2. Add the strawberries and let sit for 10 minutes.

3. Add the salad greens and pecans, and toss.

4. Top with cheese and serve immediately.

Easy Three-Bean Salad

Beans have been linked with magick for centuries, and some traditions say beans have the power to make wishes come true—especially wishes involving love. The number three represents manifestation, so this deceptively simple dish is actually an edible spell to bring your dreams into the physical world. Part of this salad's power comes from the combination of its colors: black, which represents feminine power and nighttime; white, which symbolizes masculine energy and daylight; and red, which signifies passion.

YIELDS 6 SERVINGS

Tools and Ingredients

1 (15-ounce) can black beans

1 (15-ounce) can white (navy) beans

1 (15-ounce) can red kidney beans

A large mixing bowl

¾ cup chopped red onion

2 cloves garlic, finely chopped

¾ cup chopped red bell pepper

¾ cup frozen corn, thawed

½ cup olive oil

3 tablespoons red wine vinegar

Salt and pepper to taste

A wooden spoon

¼ cup chopped fresh parsley

1. Rinse the beans and put them in the mixing bowl.

2. Add the vegetables, oil, vinegar, and salt and pepper.

3. Stir to combine, using a clockwise motion, while you recite this incantation (or one you compose yourself):

> *"Dark and light, black and white*
> *Blend with red and love ignite.*
> *By the law of three times three*
> *My magick brings true love to me."*

4. Allow the bean salad to sit, covered, overnight in the fridge to meld its flavors and magickal energies before eating.

The Modern Witchcraft Book of Love Spells

Creamy Potato Salad

This recipe draws upon color correspondences as well as mythology for its potency. Red, as you know, represents passion —don't use ordinary white potatoes or peel these red beauties when you concoct this edible spell. The love goddesses Venus, Aphrodite, and Hera are said to be fond of tomatoes, whose plump redness reminds us of the heart. According to Greek folklore, the olive tree is considered sacred to the Greek goddess Athena, and eating olives ensures fertility. If you want to add protein to this salad, you can include two chopped hardboiled eggs, which also symbolize fertility.

YIELDS 4 SERVINGS

Tools and Ingredients

4 cups cooked red-skin potatoes, cooled and cut into pieces

A large mixing bowl

⅓ cup mayonnaise

¼ cup plain Greek-style yogurt

2 tablespoons Dijon mustard

Juice of 1 lime

Salt and pepper to taste

1 medium tomato, chopped

1 can (2¼ ounces) sliced black olives, drained

3 scallions, snipped

1. Put the cooled potatoes in the bowl; add the mayonnaise, yogurt, mustard, lime juice, salt, and pepper. Stir in a clockwise direction until potatoes are covered.
2. Add the tomato and olives, and stir.
3. Sprinkle the scallions on top and chill at least 1 hour before serving.

SEXY SEAFOOD DISHES

Asian-Style Oysters

The ancient Greeks believed oysters stirred the libido—remember Botticelli's painting of the love goddess Aphrodite washing ashore on an oyster shell? Enjoy this lusty oyster dish with a lover to spark romance.

YIELDS 2 SERVINGS

Tools and Ingredients

8 oysters, grilled until shells open

A plate or platter

6–8 shiitake mushrooms, diced

3 scallion greens, snipped into small circles

1 tablespoon grated fresh ginger

3 tablespoons sesame oil

2 ounces soy sauce

A small saucepan

1. Arrange the grilled oysters in their shells on the plate or platter.
2. Sprinkle with the mushrooms, scallions, and ginger.
3. Heat the sesame oil and soy sauce in a saucepan, and then pour over the oysters and serve.

Shrimp and Saffron Rice

The custom of showering a newlywed couple with rice dates back to ancient Rome, and is said to bring prosperity, fertility, and good fortune. Spicy golden saffron is sometimes added to talismans to increase passion—and it brings a lusty zing to this recipe too. Share this colorful dish with a lover.

YIELDS 4 SERVINGS

Tools and Ingredients

2½ cups cooked saffron rice

16 medium-sized shrimp, cooked, with tails removed

2 hardboiled eggs, chopped

Salad bowl and tongs

Red grapes, halved

1 cucumber, peeled, seeded, and cut into bite-sized pieces

¾ cup chopped pecans or walnuts

Your favorite mayonnaise (or other) dressing

Spring mix or other mixed salad greens

1. Chill the cooked rice, shrimp, and eggs in a salad bowl.
2. Add the grapes, cucumber, and nuts; dress with mayonnaise or other dressing and combine.
3. Serve over a bed of mixed salad greens.

Saffron's Medicinal Magick

Saffron, which comes from a type of crocus flower, has been prized for its healing and magickal properties since ancient times. A 3,500-year-old fresco at Thíra, Greece, depicts a goddess directing the manufacture of a saffron-based medication. Today the golden spice is showing hopeful signs as a treatment for Alzheimer's disease, depression, MS, liver and heart problems, and many other ailments.

Baked Honeyed Salmon

Not only is salmon rich in healthy omega-3 oils, but its pretty pink color symbolizes affection and romance. Add some sweet honey and a dash of spicy mustard and you've got a potent combination for love.

YIELDS 2 SERVINGS

Tools and Ingredients

1 pound organic, wild-caught
  salmon

A baking pan

2 tablespoons butter

2 teaspoons spicy brown mustard

2 teaspoons honey

2 tablespoons dry white wine

A small saucepan

A small basting brush

1. Preheat oven to 400°F.
2. Lay the salmon, skin down, on a baking pan (on aluminum foil, if you prefer, for easy cleanup).
3. Heat the other ingredients in the saucepan until melted. Brush the mixture on the salmon.
4. Bake about 15 minutes, checking periodically to make sure the fish isn't getting overdone (it should still be bright pink and moist when you flake it with a fork).

Vesica Piscis

The symbol known as the vesica piscis represents the female genitalia and, by extension, feminine power. The symbol, sometimes called the vessel of the fish, dates back to matriarchal cultures and often appeared at sites considered holy to followers of goddess-centered religions. Today, many Christians take this symbol as a sign of their religion without understanding its earlier roots.

Crabmeat in Avocado Halves

The crab is the symbol for the zodiac sign Cancer, ruled by the moon, the heavenly body witches connect with the Goddess and the emotions. Halved avocados, with their womblike shape (after the seed is removed), echo the fertile, feminine nature of this delicious and healthy salad.

YIELDS 2 SERVINGS

Tools and Ingredients

1 egg yolk	½ pound pink lump crabmeat
1 teaspoon spicy brown mustard	Salad greens
¼ teaspoon Worcestershire sauce	2 salad plates
1 teaspoon white wine vinegar	2 ripe avocados, halved, seeds
2 mixing bowls	removed
A wire whisk	Lemon juice
¼ cup sesame oil	2 hardboiled eggs, cut into quarters
½ teaspoon cocktail sauce	⅛ cup finely sliced scallion greens
Salt and pepper to taste	Red onion rings

1. Put the egg yolk, mustard, Worcestershire sauce, and vinegar in one of the mixing bowls and whisk until smooth. Add the oil and continue whisking until it starts to thicken.

2. Add cocktail sauce and salt and pepper to taste; continue whisking until smooth.

3. Put the crabmeat in the other mixing bowl. Pour half the sauce over it and combine.

4. Arrange salad greens on the plates. Place two avocado halves on each plate, peel down, and sprinkle with lemon juice to keep the avocado from darkening.

5. Spoon the crabmeat mixture on top of the avocado halves, and then pour the rest of the sauce over everything.

6. Arrange the hardboiled egg quarters around the avocado halves. Sprinkle with scallions and lay onion rings on top of the crabmeat. Serve chilled.

DIVINE DESSERTS

Strawberries with Chocolate Sauce

This quick-and-easy treat combines three sweet ingredients witches associate with love: strawberries, chocolate, and sugar. Eat the berries yourself or invite a lover to share.

YIELDS 2 SERVINGS

Tools and Ingredients

12 fresh strawberries

4 ounces dark chocolate

A small saucepan

A plate

Confectioners' sugar

1. Wash the strawberries, leaving the stems on.
2. Slowly melt the chocolate in a small saucepan, stirring in a clockwise direction until smooth.
3. Dip the strawberries, one by one, into the chocolate so that about ¾ of each berry is coated.
4. Lay the berries on a plate and sprinkle with sugar.

Fruit of the Goddess

Apples and peaches are among the favorite foods of Venus, the Roman goddess of love. Make this delicious dessert for your beloved and enjoy eating it together.

YIELDS 1 (9") PIE

Tools and Ingredients

A small bowl

⅓ packed cup light brown sugar

⅓ cup granulated sugar

2 rounded tablespoons all-purpose flour

½ teaspoon ground cinnamon

¼ teaspoon ground nutmeg

⅛ teaspoon salt

3 tart apples, peeled, cored, and sliced

3 fresh peaches, peeled, seeded, and sliced

A paring knife

A 9" piecrust in a pie pan

2 tablespoons butter or margarine

1. Preheat oven to 425°F.
2. Combine all the dry ingredients in a small bowl.
3. Arrange half of the fruit slices in the piecrust, and then sprinkle half the sugar mixture over the fruit. Dot with half the butter.
4. Repeat, using the rest of the fruit, sugar mix, and butter.
5. As you work, say aloud:

> *"Sweeten our love,*
> *With blessings from above."*

6. Bake about 45–50 minutes or until the fruit and crust are lightly browned. (Cover with foil for part of the time if the crust seems to be cooking too fast.)

Strawberry-Rhubarb Pie

Plump, red, heart-shaped strawberries symbolize love. If possible, use fresh strawberries and rhubarb for this sweet-and-tangy pie, but if they're not available frozen fruit will work fine (defrost and blot excess water with paper towels before using).

YIELDS 1 (9") PIE

Tools and Ingredients

A small bowl

1 cup granulated sugar (more if you like it sweeter)

4–6 tablespoons all-purpose flour

¼ teaspoon salt

2 (9") piecrusts

A 9" pie pan

2 cups quartered fresh (or frozen) strawberries

2 cups 1"-pieces fresh (or frozen) rhubarb

A paring knife

A fork

1. Preheat oven to 425°F.
2. In bowl, combine the dry ingredients.
3. Place one of the piecrusts in the pie pan. Arrange half the fruit on the piecrust, and then sprinkle with half the dry ingredients; repeat.
4. Carefully lay the second piecrust on top of the fruit. Gently draw a heart in the top piecrust by piercing it with a fork.
5. Bake about 45–50 minutes or until the crust is lightly browned and fruit juice is bubbling through the heart pattern. (Cover with foil for part of the time if the crust seems to be cooking too fast.)

Charmed Chocolate Cake

Chocolate has long been connected with love—that's why people give chocolates on Valentine's Day. This delicious cake has an added ingredient, however: a love charm.

YIELDS 1 (9") TWO-LAYER CAKE

Tools and Ingredients

3 pink or red roses in a vase
A bell
A medium mixing bowl
A large mixing bowl
2 cups sifted all-purpose flour
1 teaspoon baking soda
½ teaspoon salt
½ cup shortening, softened
1 cup granulated sugar
Electric mixer
2 large eggs, beaten

3 squares unsweetened chocolate, melted
¾ teaspoon vanilla extract
½ teaspoon peppermint extract
1 cup whole milk
2 (9") round cake pans, lined with wax paper and greased
Your favorite frosting (chocolate, butter cream, etc.)
6 pink or red cake candles
Matches or a lighter

1. Place the roses on the kitchen counter where you can see them while you work. Set the bell nearby.

2. Preheat oven to 350°F.

3. In the medium bowl combine the flour, baking soda, and salt. In the large mixing bowl combine the shortening and sugar with the electric mixer.

4. After you complete each step of this recipe, ring the bell and repeat the following incantation (or one you compose yourself) to "charm" the cake:

"Love come my way.
Be mine today.
Love come to stay.
Forever I pray."

5. Add the eggs to the shortening mixture and blend, and then add the melted chocolate and blend.

6. Stir the vanilla and peppermint extracts into the milk.

7. Alternate adding ⅓ of the milk and then ⅓ of the flour to the shortening mixture, blending until smooth, until all the milk and flour are combined into the shortening mixture.

8. Pour the batter into the cake pans and bake 25–30 minutes or until done.

9. Allow the cakes to cool, and then remove the layers from their pans. Put one layer on top of the other and frost the cake.

10. Top with pink or red candles.

11. Set the vase of roses on the table when you serve the cake. Light the candles and make a wish before blowing them out.

"Magic . . . uses all of reality, the world itself, as its medium."
—BILL WHITCOMB, *THE MAGICIAN'S COMPANION*

Chapter 9

SPELLS TO HONOR THE SEASONS AND SPECIAL DAYS

Did you know that many of the holidays we celebrate today have their roots in the special dates marked by the early Greeks, Romans, Celts, and Germanic peoples of northern Europe? For centuries we have observed the sun's apparent passage through the sky and its effects on earth. Our ancestors thought of this annual cycle as the journey of the Sun King as he drove his chariot across the heavens.

Decorate Your Altar Seasonally

Mark the equinoxes and solstices by decorating your altar anew at each season. Placing flowers, greenery, dried fruit, and nuts on your altar is a common and colorful custom. You might also want to display an image of a deity who's associated with the season; for example, Artemis in the spring, Isis in the summer, Demeter in the fall, and Sophia in wintertime.

Pagans and Wiccans call the cycle the Wheel of the Year and divide it into eight periods of approximately six weeks each. Each "spoke" in the Wheel corresponds to a holiday, or "sabbat." Four of the sabbats are linked to the sun's entrance into the cardinal signs of the zodiac:

- The Spring Equinox, or Ostara, occurs on the day the sun reaches 0 degrees of Aries.
- The Summer Solstice, or Midsummer, coincides with the sun's ingress into Cancer.
- The Fall Equinox, or Mabon, is celebrated when the sun enters Libra.
- The Winter Solstice, or Yule, marks the first day of Capricorn.

The other four sabbats fall at the halfway points between the equinoxes and solstices. Called the "cross-quarter" days, because they come at the midpoints of the seasons, these festivals are known to pagans as Samhain, Imbolc, Beltane, and Lughnassadh. (In my book *The Modern Guide to Witchcraft* you can read more about the sabbats, their history, significance, and ways to celebrate them.)

Each of these special days affords unique opportunities for performing magick. The sabbats aren't the only special dates to mark with magickal workings, however. Your birthday is one of the most auspicious days to celebrate. You'll also want to observe births, deaths, weddings, and anniversaries of important life events.

"The sabbats mainly honor the Goddess in her aspect of mother earth and the God in his forms of solar king and vegetation god."
—ARIN MURPHY-HISCOCK, SOLITARY WICCA FOR LIFE

The Modern Witchcraft Book of Love Spells

SAMHAIN SPELL TO REMOVE AN OBSTACLE TO LOVE

Considered to be the witches' New Year, Samhain (pronounced "SOW-een") begins the Wheel of the Year and is usually observed on the night of October 31. (The word *samhain* is Irish, meaning "summer's end.") Because this sabbat marks the end of the old year and the start of the new one, it's a good time to let go of old attitudes, behaviors, and baggage that may be interfering with a relationship—sort of like making a New Year's resolution.

Tools and Ingredients

A black piece of paper

A pen that writes silver ink

Pine essential oil

A cauldron or flameproof pot

Matches or a lighter

Dried sage leaves

1. On the paper, write at least one thing you intend to release in order to improve your relationship. It may be jealousy, stubbornness, fear of commitment, a need to always be right—whatever you feel is standing in the way of your happiness.

2. When you've finished, dot essential oil at each corner of the paper and fold it three times.

3. Hold the paper over the cauldron or pot, light the paper, and drop it into the vessel.

4. Sprinkle the sage leaves on the burning paper. As you watch the flame, envision the unwanted obstacle to your happiness burning up too.

YULE TREE MAGICK

Yule (the Winter Solstice) is celebrated when the sun reaches 0 degrees of the zodiac sign Capricorn, usually around December 21. This is the shortest day of the year in the Northern Hemisphere. Although many people associate decorating evergreen trees with Christmas, the custom is rooted in ancient pagan tradition and wasn't adopted by Christians until the Victorian era. Because evergreens retain their needles even during the cold winter months, they symbolize the triumph of life over death.

Tools and Ingredients

Objects that represent your intentions

A live evergreen tree

Rosewater (see Chapter 4)

1. Collect objects that represent your intentions: to attract new love, to increase romance in an existing relationship, to strengthen a commitment, etc. For example, if one of your intentions is to take a trip with your lover, you could use a toy airplane to symbolize your wish.

2. Position the tree in your home and decorate it with the objects you've selected. As you hang each object on the tree, focus on its meaning and symbolism for you. Envision whatever it represents manifesting in your life.

3. Water the tree with rosewater and thank the tree for lending its energy to help fulfill your intentions.

4. Leave the decorations on the tree for as long as you like. When you take them down, store them in a box until next year, when you'll see how many of your wishes came true during the year.

5. Plant the tree outside, or continue to care for it in your home.

IMBOLC CREATIVITY SPELL

This sabbat honors Brigid, the beloved Celtic goddess of poetry, healing, and smithcraft. Also known as Candlemas, the holiday usually begins on the evening of January 31 and concludes on February 2. Choose candles for you and your lover in colors you like or that correspond to your zodiac birth signs. The other candles should be in colors that correspond to your intentions (see Chapter 6).

Tools and Ingredients

A candle, in a holder, to represent you

A candle, in a holder, to represent your lover

A candle, in a holder, to represent each of your intentions

Matches or a lighter

A greeting card with an envelope

A pen that writes red ink

An athame, nail file, or other pointed tool

1. Place the candles on your altar and light them.

2. On the greeting card, write a poem to your lover that expresses the intentions you've assigned to the candles. You needn't be a poet laureate—your poem doesn't even need to rhyme. Your sincerity and caring are what matter. As you write, hold your intentions in your mind and keep love in your heart.

3. When you've finished, slip the card in the envelope. Pick up the candle that represents you, tilt it slightly, and drip some of the wax onto the envelope to seal it.

4. Let the wax cool somewhat, but not harden. With your athame (or other pointed tool) inscribe a sigil you design to honor your love. Allow the candles to finish burning down completely.

5. Give the poem to your lover.

SOW SEEDS OF LOVE ON OSTARA

Pagans and witches celebrate Ostara when the sun enters 0 degrees of Aries, around March 21. Ostara gets its name from the German fertility goddess Ostare; the word *Easter* derives from the same root. The Spring Equinox marks the first day of spring and the start of the planting season in agrarian cultures (in the Northern Hemisphere).

Tools and Ingredients

A flowerpot or other container

A crystal or gemstone that represents your intention, cleansed (see Chapter 3)

Potting soil

Seeds of a plant that represents your intention (see Chapter 4)

Rosewater (see Chapter 4)

1. In the bottom of the flowerpot or other container place the crystal or gemstone you've chosen.
2. Fill the flowerpot with potting soil.
3. Sow the seeds you've chosen into the soil. Keep your mind focused on your intention as you work.
4. Water with the rosewater as you say aloud this incantation (or one you compose yourself):

> *"Now I sow these seeds of love*
> *While the sun shines up above;*
> *Mother Earth supports the growth*
> *Of blessings water doth bring forth.*
> *Thus the elements conspire*
> *To bring about all I desire."*

5. Continue caring for the seeds you've planted. Enjoy watching as they sprout and your wishes bloom.

DANCE AROUND A MAYPOLE

Witches usually celebrate Beltane, another fertility holiday, on May 1; it coincides with a time of fruitfulness when crops sprout in the fields and baby animals are born. The sabbat is named for the god Baal, sometimes called "the bright one." Rituals performed on this day often include sexual symbolism—the Maypole in this one is obviously phallic.

Tools and Ingredients

A washtub, large bucket, or other container

Cement or other type of mortar

Water

Ribbons in various colors, one for each person participating in the ritual; each ribbon should be 12' long

A pole about 7' tall

A wreath of flowers

1. Begin a day or so before you'll enact the dance. In the washtub or other container, mix the cement and water.

2. Tie or otherwise affix the ribbons to the top of the Maypole. Position the pole in the cement and allow it to set.

3. Invite each person who wants to participate to form a circle around the Maypole and grasp a ribbon. (Traditionally, young virgins danced around the Maypole, but today anyone can join in.)

4. Organize yourselves so that every other person dances in a clockwise direction; the rest dance in a counterclockwise direction.

5. Alternate lifting your ribbon above and then below that of each person you meet as you circle around the Maypole. Your ribbons will wrap around the pole and create a pretty interwoven pattern. (You can view this on YouTube to get a better idea of how the process works.)

6. When you've finished twining the ribbons around the pole, a woman who seeks a romantic relationship tosses a circular garland over the top of the pole, signifying the sex act as a way of asking the Goddess to send her a lover. Singing, drumming, and other forms of merriment can enrich this age-old ritual.

COMMUNE WITH NATURE SPIRITS AT MIDSUMMER

In the Northern Hemisphere, the Summer Solstice is the longest day of the year. Witches generally celebrate Midsummer around June 21, when the sun enters 0 degrees of the zodiac sign Cancer. This spell lets you gain assistance from the elementals, the nonphysical beings who enliven the four elements: earth, air, fire, and water.

Tools and Ingredients

A green gemstone (such as jade, malachite, aventurine, or emerald; see
    Chapter 3), cleansed

A feather

A red votive candle

A vial of essential oil that relates to your intention

A tarot card that represents your intention

Matches or a lighter

1. On your altar or another surface, place the gemstone in the north, the feather in the east, the candle in the south, and the essential oil in the west.
2. Place the tarot card face-up in the center of the square you've configured with the other items.

3. Light the candle and focus on your intention, as you say this incantation (or one you compose yourself) aloud:

> *"Elementals shining bright*
> *Come on this Midsummer's night.*
> *Gnomes, bring earthly pleasures dear.*
> *Sylphs, make conversation clear.*
> *Salamanders, spark desire.*
> *Undines, set our hearts on fire.*
> *On this blessed and magick day*
> *Love and joy now come my way."*

4. Envision the intention you've designed, signified by the tarot card, manifesting in your life as you sense the elementals coming to your aid. You may see these beings or sense them in another way.

5. Tell them you are offering the gifts on your altar (the stone, feather, candle, and essential oil) in exchange for the elementals' assistance. Explain what you need and want them to do. You may sense a response that lets you know they've agreed to help you.

6. Leave the items in place for three days and light the candle for a few minutes each day. At the end of that time, release your attachment to an outcome and allow the elementals to aid in its manifestation.

Become Invisible

Folklore says that if you wish to become invisible you must wear an amulet that includes seeds collected from forest ferns on Midsummer's Eve. Of course, you won't really disappear, but the amulet will shield you from the prying eyes of others so you can go about your affairs undetected.

KITCHEN WITCH SPELL FOR LUGHNASSADH

Named for the Irish Celtic god Lugh, Lughnassadh (pronounced "LOO-na-saad") is the first of the harvest festivals, usually celebrated on August 1. The early Christians dubbed the holiday Lammas, meaning "loaf-mass," because grain was cut at this time of the year and made into bread. Kitchen witches seek to nurture their families (and extended community) spiritually and physically; therefore, food often plays a central role in their magick work.

Tools and Ingredients

Tools and ingredients to make your favorite bread recipe

A small dried bean

1. As you knead the dough, add the dried bean. Hold loving thoughts in your mind while you work and project them into the dough.
2. Bake and serve the bread to friends and loved ones. Whoever gets the bean in his or her portion will be granted a wish.

Magick Beans

Remember the fairy tale about Jack and the Beanstalk? Although published in England in the early eighteenth century, the story dates back as far as 5,000 years ago. The tale is based on a long-standing belief that beans have magickal properties.

MABON FRUIT BASKET SPELL FOR HARMONY

The Autumn Equinox, also known as the harvest festival Mabon, usually occurs on or about September 22, when the sun reaches 0 degrees of Libra. Day and night are of equal length, signifying a time of balance, equality, and harmony. Libra is ruled by Venus, the planet of love and relationships, so this is an ideal time to do love spells.

Tools and Ingredients

4 ribbons—1 red, 1 blue, 1 yellow, 1 green—long enough to wind around a basket's handle

A pen or marker that writes on fabric

Rosewater (see Chapter 4)

A basket with a handle

Fruit that symbolizes love and harmony (see Chapter 8)

1. On each ribbon write a blessing or affirmation that expresses love, peace, and harmony. The ribbons' colors represent the four elements: red = fire, blue = water, yellow = air, and green = earth.

2. Dot each ribbon with rosewater, and then wind the ribbons around the handle of the basket. As you work, recite aloud the affirmations written on the ribbons.

3. Fill the basket with the fruit you've chosen. As you place each item in the basket, contemplate its meaning. For example, apples are sacred to the Goddess and symbolize love; blueberries signify tranquility.

4. Place the basket on your altar or dining table. Share the fruit with your lover to support harmony in your relationship.

BIRTHDAY MAGICK

Your birthday is one of the best days of the year for doing magick, when positive celestial energies favor you. This spell is a variation on the familiar birthday cake tradition.

Tools and Ingredients

Tools and ingredients to make a cake

Candles in holders

Matches or a lighter

1. Bake a cake of a flavor that corresponds to your intention; for example, chocolate for romance, spice for passion and excitement, vanilla for harmony and cooperation.

2. Add the digits of your age together and reduce to a single digit to determine how many candles to use for this spell. For example, if you are twenty-four at this birthday, add 2 + 4 to get 6—you'll need six candles. If you end up with a double-digit number, add those numbers together until you get a single-digit number. Let's say you're nineteen: 1 + 9 = 10, so then add 1 + 0 = 1. Usually, numerologists leave numbers 11 and 22 as is; however, if that many candles would be cumbersome, you can reduce the number to 2 or 4. Choose colors that correspond to your intentions (see Chapter 6).

3. Assign a wish to each candle and set the candles on your dining table. As you light each candle, say your wish aloud.

4. Enjoy eating the cake, alone or with your partner, and/or other people.

5. Allow the candles to burn down completely instead of blowing them out to make your wishes come true.

SPELL TO BLESS A NEW BABY

If you've recently given birth or know someone who has, do this spell to bring the child good fortune. As a baby gift, you might consider having an astrological reading done for the newborn—this can help the parents understand their child's unique abilities and how they can nurture them.

Tools and Ingredients

A birth chart for the baby

A clear quartz crystal (cleansed)

1. Cast or acquire a birth chart for the baby, based on the date, time, and place of his or her birth. (You can order the chart online from www.astro.com or other services.)

2. Print the chart and lay it face-up on your altar or another surface.

3. Set the crystal in the center of the horoscope wheel and leave it in place overnight.

4. If this spell is for your own baby, place the crystal on a windowsill in the child's room to bring good fortune. If you did the spell for someone else's baby, give the crystal and the chart to the mother.

The Horoscope Wheel

A birth chart or horoscope is a two-dimensional representation of the heavens at the moment of birth, as viewed from the place of birth. It looks like a wheel with twelve sections, occupied by symbols that signify the positions of the celestial bodies.

NEW MOON SPELL TO BRING LUCK IN LOVE

This spell infuses a new relationship with good energy to help it develop happily. The spell is based on a magick square, a configuration of small, numbered squares arranged in rows and columns in such a way that the numbers in each column and row add up to the same sum.

4	9	2
3	5	7
8	1	6

Tools and Ingredients

9 gemstones that represent what you desire in a new relationship
(see Chapter 3), cleansed
A magick square of Saturn, drawn on paper
A dark blue cloth

1. Choose nine gemstones that symbolize what you seek in a budding relationship. For example, rose quartz for romance and affection, carnelian for passion, jade for joy and loyalty.

2. On the night of the new moon, draw a magick square of Saturn on paper and lay it on your altar (or other surface).

3. Decide which of your wishes is most important, and then lay the gemstone that corresponds to that wish on the square numbered 1. State your intention aloud.

4. Do the same with each wish and each square until you've positioned all nine gemstones on the squares.

5. Cover the configuration with a dark blue cloth that signifies the night sky. Allow the magickal energies you've called into being to remain, contained and nurtured, overnight.

6. In the morning uncover the configuration and either leave the stones on your altar (remove the square) or carry them with you until all nine wishes come true.

FULL MOON SPELL TO CELEBRATE YOUR LOVE

The full moon is a time of fulfillment and manifestation. With this spell you rejoice in your love and mark the joy between you and your partner.

Tools and Ingredients

9 gemstones that represent things you value in your relationship (see Chapter 3), cleansed

9 ivory-colored candles in candleholders

Essential oil that represents your intentions

Matches or a lighter

1. Choose nine gemstones whose energies symbolize things you prize in your relationship; for example, carnelian corresponds to passion, hematite to commitment, moonstone to acceptance.

2. Position the candles in holders in a circle on your altar (or another surface).

3. Dot each candle with essential oil, starting with the one in the easternmost position and working clockwise around the circle.

4. Lay the gemstones in the center of the circle of candles.

5. Beginning in the east, light the candles in a clockwise direction as you reflect on all the good things in your relationship.

6. Allow the candles to burn down as you give thanks for the blessings you've enjoyed in your relationship thus far and those you intend to receive in the future.

BLESSING TO HONOR A DECEASED LOVER

This blessing honors a lover (or other loved one) who has left the physical world and gone to the world beyond this one that witches call the Summerland. The spell calls to mind the myth of crossing the River Styx into the afterlife.

Tools and Ingredients

A white candle in a holder

Matches or a lighter

A piece of tree bark (from a sacred tree if possible; see Chapter 4)

A pen or marker that writes black ink

Rose essential oil

A leaf

A small stone

A piece of biodegradable string

1. Set the candle on your altar or another surface and light it.
2. On the smooth (inner) side of the bark, write the name of the person who has gone to the afterlife and say a blessing for him or her.
3. Draw a heart around the name and dot the bark with essential oil.
4. Write the blessing on the leaf. Lay the leaf and the stone on the bark, and tie them in place with the string.
5. Extinguish the candle. Take the bark to a body of moving water: a stream, river, or ocean (during the ebbing tide). Place the bark boat in the water and repeat the blessing as the boat floats away.

"You are always nearer to the divine and the true sources of your power than you think. . . . Every place is under the stars, every place is the center of the world."

—John Burroughs, *Studies in Nature and Literature*

Chapter 10

SPELLS AND RITUALS TO DO WITH A PARTNER

Performing spells and rituals with your partner is a wonderful way to honor your relationship. It also doubles the power you bring to a love spell. Of course, it's possible your beloved doesn't want to get involved in magick work—he or she may be skeptical about all this witchy stuff or might not even know you're into it. If your lover is interested in sharing magickal experiences with you, however, the spells and rituals in this chapter are for you.

> *"Love is the light in which we see each thing in its true origin, image, nature, and destiny. Unless you see someone or something in the light of love, you do not see them or it at all."*
> —SIRONA KNIGHT, *LOVE, SEX, AND MAGICK*

TOAST YOUR LOVE

According to the *International Handbook on Alcohol and Culture,* raising glasses in a toast recalls the ancient tradition of offering sacred libations to the goddesses and gods in hopes of receiving favors from them.

Tools and Ingredients

Wine, champagne, or sparking apple cider

2 chalices (or wineglasses)

1. Pour the beverage into your chalices (or glasses).

2. Raise your chalices and toast to your love. As you clink chalices (or glasses), say aloud:

> *"Lord and Lady so divine,*
> *By your hands our hearts entwine."*

3. Sip the beverage while you concentrate on sending loving energy to your partner.

Aleister Crowley and the Practice of Sex Magick

Magick's notorious bad boy, English occultist Aleister Crowley, did much to promote and influence the course sex magick has taken in the West. Crowley learned sex magick while traveling in India and Africa, and he emphasized its practice through the organization he headed, the Ordo Templi Orientis (O.T.O.).

CAST A CIRCLE TOGETHER

Casting a circle before doing a spell or ritual is a basic practice witches use (discussed in Chapter 1), and there are many ways to cast a protective circle around the place where you perform magick. You cast this one together, drawing upon the four elements to assist you.

Tools and Ingredients

A stick of incense, preferably sage

Matches or a lighter

A bowl of salt water

1. Decide which of you will cast with incense and which with salt water. In a male-female relationship, usually the man holds the incense and the woman sprinkles the water.

2. Begin in the east. One person lights a stick of incense and begins walking clockwise around the perimeter of the circle where you will be working, trailing the fragrant smoke behind so that both of you are inside the circle. He or she says aloud: "With fire and air I cast this magick circle."

3. When that person has finished, the other person walks the perimeter of the circle clockwise again, this time sprinkling salt water to cast the circle. He or she says aloud: "With water and earth I cast this magick circle."

4. Now you're ready to enact your spell or ritual within the circle.

"In Witchcraft, we define a new space and a new time whenever we cast a circle to begin a ritual. The circle exists on the boundaries of ordinary space and time; it is 'between the worlds' of the seen and unseen . . . a space within which alternate realities meet, in which the past and future are open to us."

—STARHAWK, *THE SPIRAL DANCE*

BASK IN AN HERBAL LOVE BATH

Ritual baths have long been a part of magickal practice. Bathing relaxes your mind and body, and helps shift your consciousness to a higher plane. Soak in this herbal bath together as a prelude to another spell or ritual, or as a spell in itself.

Tools and Ingredients

1 cup Epsom or sea salts
Lavender essential oil
Several sprigs of fresh rosemary
A pink candle in a holder
Matches or a lighter

1. While you run comfortably hot water in your bathtub, pour the Epsom or sea salts into the water.

2. Add six drops of lavender essential oil to the water, and then add the sprigs of fresh rosemary. (Rub the rosemary between your palms beforehand to release its lovely scent.)

3. Turn off all electric lights, light the candle, and then get into the bath.

4. Relax in the warm water as you inhale the pleasant scents of rosemary and lavender. Invite loving energies to surround and infuse you. Allow all worries and stress to wash away, into the soothing bathwater.

5. Soak for as long as you like. When you feel ready, emerge from your bath relaxed, balanced, and confident of your ability to give and receive love fully. Remove the rosemary. Extinguish the candle and let the bathwater flow down the drain, taking all your concerns away with it.

"The way to health is to have an aromatic bath and a scented massage every day."

—HIPPOCRATES

THE FIVE-FOLD KISS

In this ritual, you honor and bless one another. You may enact this as a greeting and expression of endearment, or the ritual may precede a ceremony such as a handfasting. Although the wording here is for a male-female couple, same-sex couples may perform the ritual too.

Tools and Ingredients

None

1. The woman stands and the man kneels in front of her as he says: "Blessed are your feet for they have brought you to me." He then kisses her feet.

2. Next, he says: "Blessed are your knees that let you kneel at the sacred altar." He kisses her knees.

3. Next, he says: "Blessed is your womb, for it brings life into the world." He kisses her abdomen.

4. He stands and says: "Blessed are your breasts, which nourish life." He kisses her breasts.

5. Next, he says: "Blessed are your lips that utter the names of the Goddess and God." He kisses her on the lips.

6. Now the woman blesses the man, kneeling before him while he stands. She repeats the blessing, changing the words so they're sex specific; for example, in step 3 change "womb" to "penis" and in step 4 say, "Blessed is your chest that holds your heart." She enacts the same gestures.

A more intimate version of this ritual is given in my book *Sex Magic for Beginners.*

HANDFASTING RITUAL

In Celtic tradition handfasting is a temporary marriage that lasts a year and a day. At the end of that time, the couple can decide to make the marriage permanent or part company. You and your partner can perform a handfasting ritual yourselves or ask someone else to officiate.

Tools and Ingredients

Flowers of your choice

A pink candle in a holder

Images of a paired goddess and god of your choice (for example, Isis and Osiris)

Sage leaves in a ceramic bowl or shell

Matches or a lighter

Rings

Gold and silver cords long enough to wrap loosely around your wrists

An athame

A chalice

1. On your altar, set the flowers, candle, and images of the god and goddess you've chosen to bless you in this ritual.

2. Smudge each other with the burning sage. (If someone is officiating, he or she should do the smudging and if any guests are present at the ceremony, smudge them too.)

3. Cast a circle. The circle may enclose all who are in attendance or only the couple and/or the person officiating (your choice).

4. Light the candle and face east as you say: "We invoke the spirits of air, you who dwell in the land of sunrise. Bear witness to this rite as we exchange the sacred kiss. May the realm of new beginnings bless us with unity. We bid you hail and welcome."

5. Face south and say: "We invoke the spirits of fire who dwell in the land of high noon. Bless us with the creative aspects of your nature. May the warm glow of true love be ours. We bid you hail and welcome."

6. Face west and say: "We invoke the spirits of water who dwell in the land of sunset. Cleanse us with your waves that all doubt be washed away, and may our joy overflow. We bid you hail and welcome."

7. Face north and say: "We invoke the spirits of the earth who dwell in the land of midnight. Stand with us firm and true as our souls unite in harmonious accord. May our bond be strong and hold fast for the time of our choosing. We bid you hail and welcome."

8. Ask the goddess and the god, represented by the images you've chosen, to bear witness to the handfasting. Ask them to bless the union, to guide, protect, and aid you for as long as you walk together.

9. Exchange rings, and say: "I join with you and offer this ring as a symbol of my pledge and of the light that love brings to our life together."

10. Cross your arms at the wrists and clasp hands. If someone else is officiating, he or she loosely wraps the gold and silver cords around your wrists. If you are performing the ritual yourselves, you may need to wrap the cords around your wrists first and then join hands. Say aloud:

"By sun and moon   *We shall not part*
Earth and sea   *For a year and a day.*
I bind to you   *May our union*
And you to me.   *Blessed be."*
Neither to go
A separate way.

11. Remove the cords.

12. The man holds the athame; the woman holds the chalice. (If you are both of the same sex, choose who will hold which tool.)

13. Insert the athame, blade down, into the chalice to symbolize sexual as well as spiritual union. Say together: "So mote it be."

14. Thank and release the deities and the guardians of the four directions. Open the circle.

The statements offered here are suggestions only; consider creating your own. You may also wish to add other steps to the ritual, such as reading poetry, sharing a libation, or playing music.

Handfasting Legalities

Unless the person officiating at a handfasting is a minister, justice of the peace, or other individual qualified to perform a marriage ceremony— and you complete the required documents—a handfasting is not a legally binding arrangement.

CREATE A LOVE MANDALA

Mandalas are intricate and beautiful circular images that represent earth and heaven. The word *mandala* means "circle" in Sanskrit. Often the designs include spiritual or magickal symbols. Traditional Hindu and Buddhist mandalas are usually dedicated to a deity; however, you and your partner can create a mandala and dedicate it to your love.

Tools and Ingredients

A large piece of paper or cardboard   Colored pens, pencils, or markers

Personal photographs   Magazine pictures

Glue or tape   Scissors

1. On the paper draw a circle about 2' in diameter (larger if you wish).

2. Affix a photo of the two of you together or individual photos in the center of the circle.

3. Inside the circle, draw symbols, images, etc. that represent love or have special meaning for you.

4. From magazines, cut pictures that express love, happiness, and things you desire to bring to your relationship. For example, you could select a picture of a place you want to go on vacation together. Glue or tape these pictures inside the circle.

5. As you work, keep your attention focused on your relationship and the goal of enriching the love between you.

6. When you've finished, display the mandala where you'll see it often.

RUNE MASSAGE LOTION

This lotion gets its power from the Norse runes you add to it. Depending on your intention, you may want to choose one or more of these runes: Gebo (Gifu), Inguz, or Wunjo.

Tools and Ingredients
Red wine
A chalice or wineglass
Your favorite massage lotion (or one you make)

1. Pour some red wine into your chalice or a wineglass.

2. Pour some massage lotion into your hand.

3. Dip two fingers of your other hand into the wine, and then draw a rune in the lotion with the wine. Contemplate the meaning of the rune as you blend the wine and lotion with your fingers.

4. Massage your partner with the mixture. Continue for as long as you like, using the same rune or different ones.

5. Trade places and let your partner massage you with the infused lotion.

"Wine is the milk of Venus."

—BEN JONSON

CLEAR THE AIR

After an argument or unsettling event, you and your partner can clear the air to chase away bad vibes that might otherwise linger and interfere with your relationship. Performing this act together demonstrates your dedication to maintaining happiness and harmony.

Tools and Ingredients

Sage leaves

2 shells or ceramic bowls

Matches or a lighter

2 large feathers

1. Place the sage leaves in the shells or bowls, and light the leaves.

2. Walk through the space where the disruption occurred, using the feathers to waft and direct the smoke throughout.

3. When you've finished, stand in the center of the space and say aloud: "This space is now cleansed and cleared of all harmful, disruptive, and unbalanced energies. It is filled with divine white light, healing energy, and love. So mote it be."

KNOT MAGICK

You've probably seen nautical knots sailors tie, but you may not have known that they aren't merely utilitarian—knots also have magickal purposes. Early sailors used to symbolically tie the wind into knots on gusty days and release it by untying the knots if their ships were becalmed at sea. With this sexy spell you tie creative energy into knots and hold it until you need its power in the future.

Tools and Ingredients

A red cord

12 candles in rainbow colors, in candleholders

Matches or a lighter

1. Set an intention together, before you begin this spell. The objective is to tap the creative power of sex to fuel a magickal result.

2. Acquire a red cord that's as long as you are from the tips of your toes to the tips of your fingers when your arm is fully extended above your head.

3. Arrange the candles in a circle around the space where you will perform this spell. Enter the circle with your partner, bringing the red cord with you.

4. Cast a circle by lighting the candles, beginning in the east and continuing in a clockwise direction until all are burning.

5. Make love, coordinating your activity so that one person reaches orgasm first. At the moment of orgasm, the other person ties several knots in the cord. Then, as the second person reaches orgasm, the partner ties a few knots.

6. Throughout the entire experience, focus your minds on your objective. Your intention and energy are tied into the knots.

7. When you're finished, snuff out all the candles in a counterclockwise direction to open the circle.

8. Store the cord in a safe place until you need the creative power you tied into the knots. At that time, open one or more knots to release magickal energy that will assist you in your endeavor.

"When the sacredness of sexual union is felt, it is possible to experience your connection to the life force itself, the source of creation. This connection lifts your consciousness beyond the physical plane into a field of power and energy much greater than your own."
— Margot Anand, *The Art of Sexual Ecstasy*

SIGIL SEX SPELL

This spell uses the power of sexual pleasure to activate the secret wishes you've encoded into a magick symbol known as a sigil. See Chapter 6 as well as my book *The Modern Witchcraft Grimoire* for instructions on how to design sigils.

Tools and Ingredients
A sigil

1. With your partner, determine an intention and then draw a sigil that encodes what you seek to accomplish with this spell.
2. Place the sigil where you can see it easily—hang it on a wall or the ceiling, for instance.
3. Engage in sexual activity. At the moment of orgasm, stare at the sigil—you don't have to think about what it means; your subconscious knows even if your conscious mind is temporarily "on hold." The energy you've raised will fuel the intentions embodied in the sigil.
4. Leave the sigil in place, lay it on your altar, or put it away until another time (your choice).

THE ELIXIR OF LOVE

This loving cup includes a secret ingredient referred to as elixir. Usually the term refers to a potion with medicinal properties, but the early alchemists believed an elixir was a substance that could transform base metal into gold. In sex magick circles the term has another meaning.

Tools and Ingredients

A chalice or wineglass

Wine or apple cider

Male and female sexual fluids

1. Engage in sexual intercourse with your partner.
2. Pour some wine or apple cider in a chalice or wineglass. Add a few drops of "elixir"—the mixture of male and female sexual fluids—to the chalice.
3. Focus on each other and your love while you drink the "potentized" beverage together.

"The most powerful moment of human existence is the orgasm. Sex Magic is the art of utilizing sexual orgasm to create a reality and/or expand consciousness. All senses and psychic powers are heightened during orgasm. It is a moment when a window opens to the unlimited abundance of the unlimited universe."

—JEFFERY TYE, "TANTRA: SEX MAGIC"

CHARGE A MAGICK CHARM

Sexual fluids may also be used to charge a talisman. Sometimes called elixir in magickal circles, the mixture of male and female body fluids contains a powerful creative energy that can increase the potency of any charm, especially those intended for love or prosperity.

Tools and Ingredients

A talisman or other object you wish to charge

"Elixir"

1. Agree on an intention you wish to "birth" with this spell.
2. Engage in sexual intercourse with your partner.

3. When you've finished, collect a small amount of your mixed fluids and dab a little on a talisman. As you do this, envision your personal power activating the charm, so that it resonates with your creative energy.

4. Say the following incantation aloud (or compose one of your own):

> *"We've joined our bodies in this rite*
> *To give this magick charm great might.*
> *Charged by passion's glorious fire*
> *It brings us now our hearts' desire."*

5. Store the magick charm in a safe place until your dreams materialize.

FERTILITY RITUAL

If you want to become pregnant, this spell can help align energies for that purpose. The best time to perform it is on Beltane (May 1), the ancient festival that celebrates fertility—the spell harkens back to the time when agrarian people led livestock through Beltane fires to encourage their fertility. If you don't want to wait until the sabbat, however, consider doing the spell during the waxing moon, preferably when the moon is in Taurus or Cancer.

Tools and Ingredients

Oak logs and kindling (collect wood from sacred trees if possible; see Chapter 4)

Cedar chips

Matches or a lighter

Dried motherwort leaves

9 acorns

Fennel seeds

2 seashells

2 elongated stones

1. Using oak logs, kindling, and cedar chips, build two fires far enough apart that you can walk safely between them.

2. Drop the motherwort, acorns, and fennel into the flames.

3. Each of you holds a shell in your left hand and a stone in your right. The shell symbolizes feminine energy, the stone masculine energy.

4. Walk slowly back and forth between the fires while you envision creating a child together.

CREATE A MAGICKAL CHILD

Regardless of whether a sex act results in a flesh-and-blood child, every act produces what's known as a "magickal child." The creative energy raised during sex plants a seed in the universe, forming an etheric pattern in accordance with your intention. The outcome is later "birthed" in the physical world.

Tools and Ingredients

None

1. With your partner, design an intention. Keep it simple, and choose only one intention at a time.

2. While you engage in sex, hold an image in your minds of the outcome you intend to create.

3. At the moment of orgasm, release the image and your intention into the universe, where it will be acted on.

"For if ordinary, natural, undirected sexual intercourse can give birth to a new living being—a fairly miraculous thing in itself—then it is not terribly difficult to imagine that ritualized, intentional, willfully directed intercourse might give birth to effects of a supernatural, magical, divine (or demonic) character."

—HUGH B. URBAN, *MAGIA SEXUALIS: SEX, MAGIC, AND LIBERATION IN MODERN WESTERN ESOTERICISM*

DESIGN YOUR OWN SPELL TOGETHER

By now you've developed enough know-how to design your own original spell. Refer to the charts and lists in Chapters 3, 4, and 6 to help you choose ingredients for the spell you wish to enact.

Tools and Ingredients

Depends on your intention

1. Determine and agree on your purpose for doing the spell and the outcome you seek.
2. Determine the best time to perform the spell.
3. Write down the steps you'll include. If you'll use affirmations or incantations, compose those too.
4. Collect the ingredients you'll need, and cleanse them before using them in spellwork.
5. Depending on the spell, you may want to take a ritual bath beforehand.
6. Clean and smudge the space where you'll perform the spell.
7. Cast a circle according to your preferred method.
8. Enact the spell.
9. When you've finished, open the circle.
10. In your grimoire, record what you did and what happened. Describe the results. If necessary, adjust any parts of the spell to refine it so it will be even more effective the next time you perform it.

Chapter 11

MISCELLANEOUS SPELLS

Spellcasting, like most things, has evolved over time to keep pace with the needs, beliefs, preferences, and abilities of the people casting the spells. Early grimoires contained a lot of incantations for invoking the powers of deities and other spirits. The ancient Egyptians relied on amulets to safeguard them in the physical world and the realms beyond. In pretty much every culture, in every time and place, people have turned to wise women and men for love charms.

Today, you'll find a rich and varied assortment of magickal practices, from the homey, nature-based workings of green and hedge witches to the complex rituals of the ceremonial magicians. Whatever your reason, a spell probably exists to address it—and if you can't find one that's exactly what you're looking for, consider creating one of your own. Remember, your willpower is the most important ingredient in any spell.

"Love is the astrolabe of God's mysteries."

—Rumi

READ RUMI'S POETRY TO INCREASE LOVE

The thirteenth-century Persian Sufi poet Rumi wrote hundreds of beautiful love poems. To Sufis, human love enables us to know Divine love and Divine love is expressed through human relationships.

Tools and Ingredients

A book of Rumi's poetry

1. Each day, read one of Rumi's poems aloud while you focus on expanding your capacity to give and receive love. This practice helps to open your heart. If you wish, read Rumi's poems to your lover.

SPELL TO HEAL A BROKEN HEART

When a relationship ends, it's natural to feel sad. This spell helps ease the pain of a breakup and sets you on the path to recovery.

Tools and Ingredients

Scissors

A piece of red paper

A Band-Aid

Rosewater (see Chapter 4)

A green envelope

1. Cut a heart out of the paper, then tear the heart into two pieces.
2. Stick the pieces back together again with a Band-Aid. Say aloud: "My heart is completely healed and I am happy again."
3. Dot a little rosewater on your heart center as you envision healing energy soothing the pain. Dot some on the paper heart too.
4. Put the paper heart in the envelope and place the envelope in a bedroom drawer until your heart no longer aches.

The Modern Witchcraft Book of Love Spells

UNDO THE PAST

You really can change the past, at least on an energetic level. If you have regrets about a situation involving a lover in the past and wish you could have a "do-over," use this spell to burn up the old energetic pattern and make room for new possibilities.

Tools and Ingredients
Matches or a lighter

Frankincense incense in a holder

A piece of paper

A pen or marker that writes blue ink

A cauldron or flameproof pot

1. Light the incense and set it on your altar or other surface.

2. Close your eyes and recall a situation in the past that you would like to change energetically. Allow yourself to feel the sadness, regret, anger, or other emotion as you breathe in; then turn your head to the right and exhale quickly, casting out the emotion along with your breath. Do this three times.

3. On the paper write a description of the matter you wish to change and what you'd do instead.

4. When you've finished, hold the paper above the cauldron or pot and light it; drop the paper into the cauldron or pot. As the paper burns, feel yourself releasing guilt, suffering, anger, or another emotion associated with the matter. Let the memory of what happened dissolve and envision the situation changed according to your intention.

You may or may not actually alter the physical results of the situation; however, the energy tied to the matter will be transformed. The dynamic between you and the other person will shift, allowing forgiveness and healing to take place on a psychic level.

SPELL BOTTLE TO STABILIZE A RELATIONSHIP

Spell or "witch" bottles contain items with similar energies, brought together for a specific purpose. The bottle can be a temporary or permanent fixture, depending on your needs.

Tools and Ingredients

A dark green or brown glass bottle with a lid, cork, or stopper

A black candle in a candleholder

Matches or a lighter

White carnation petals

A spring or pinch of rosemary

4 pieces of hematite (cleansed)

4 pieces of jade (cleansed)

A photo of you and your partner together

A slip of paper

A pen or marker that writes black ink

A white ribbon

1. Wash and dry the bottle to remove any unwanted energies. If the bottle has a label, remove it.

2. Set the candle on your altar or other surface and light it.

3. Put the botanicals, gemstones, and photo in the bottle.

4. Write an affirmation that states your intention on a slip of paper and read it aloud. Roll the paper into a scroll and put it in the bottle.

5. Cap/cork the bottle and then seal it with wax dripped from the candle. Once the spell is cast, the bottle should remain sealed.

6. Tie the ribbon around the neck of the bottle, making eight knots, while you envision your intention for fidelity and devotion in your relationship.

7. Set the bottle on your altar or in the Relationship Gua of your home. If you prefer, bury the bottle in a place that's special to you.

THE GODDESS'S MAILBOX

Throughout the centuries, lovers have sought the aid of deities in matters of the heart. With this spell you ask a goddess associated with love (Venus, Aphrodite, Hathor, Freya, Isis, etc.) for help in accomplishing your objectives.

Tools and Ingredients

A heart-shaped box with a lid

A knife

Magazine pictures and/or other images

Scissors

Glue

A piece of pink paper

A pen or marker

Essential oil appropriate to your intention (see Chapter 4)

A gift for the goddess

1. Cut a slot in the lid of the box.

2. From magazines, cut pictures that represent your intention or download images from the Internet. Glue these images to the box until you've covered its surface completely.

3. On the paper, write a letter to the goddess you are petitioning for assistance. Explain your concern and ask for her help in resolving the matter. Don't beg, demand, or stipulate what you want her to do—she knows what's best for all concerned.

4. Dot each corner of the paper with essential oil, and then fold the paper three times. Write the goddess's name on the paper and slip it into the heart-shaped "mailbox" you've made.

5. Thank the goddess in advance for her help, knowing she will come to your aid. Put the gift you've chosen for her in the box. It could be a small gemstone, silver charm, or something special that relates to her personality and preferences.

TIE THE KNOT

We associate rings with love, commitment, and marriage. The phrase "tying the knot" also refers to marriage. The symbolism inherent in this spell makes it effective.

Tools and Ingredients

A piece of red or pink ribbon, 8" long

A pen or marker that writes on fabric

2 rings

A small bell with a bale or circular handle

1. On the ribbon, write your name and your partner's. Add a brief wish if you like.

2. Slide the ribbon through the rings, and then slide the ribbon through the bell's bale or handle.

3. Tie three knots in the ribbon. With each knot, recite this affirmation (or one you compose yourself): "[Lover's name] and I are now joined in perfect love and perfect trust, in harmony with Divine Will, our own true wills, and with good to all."

4. Tie the rings and bell to the knob of the door into your bedroom. Each time you open or close the door, you'll hear the tinkling of the bell and be reminded of your intention.

Ancient Wedding Rings

Five thousand years ago, the Egyptians braided hemp rings as symbols of eternal love. A married woman wore the wedding ring on what we now call the "ring finger" because supposedly a vein ran between that finger and the heart.

The Modern Witchcraft Book of Love Spells

JEALOUS LOVER SPELL

Does your beloved overreact whenever you look at or talk to someone else? If jealousy, possessiveness, and mistrust are driving a wedge between you, do this spell to help dispel your partner's insecurity and sweeten your relationship.

Tools and Ingredients

A ballpoint pen, nail, athame, or other pointed tool

A small pink pillar candle

Jasmine essential oil

A heat-resistant glass, ceramic, or metal plate

Matches or a lighter

Dried white rose petals

Dried nettle

1. With the pointed tool, inscribe your lover's name on the candle; the candle represents him or her.

2. Pour a little jasmine essential oil in your hand and dress the candle with it. Let the sweet scent soothe your mind and emotions.

3. Set the candle on the plate and light the candle.

4. Gaze at the candle and imagine you are looking at your partner. Explain your feelings and tell him or her how much you care, how important the relationship is to you. Reassure this person that you are trustworthy. Don't express anger, frustration, or criticism. Think only positive thoughts.

5. Allow the candle to burn down completely.

6. While the melted wax is still warm, crumble the rose petals and the dried nettle. Sprinkle the botanicals on the wax. Then form the soft wax into the shape of a heart.

7. Give the wax heart to your lover as a token of your affection and fidelity.

SEE NO EVIL

This spell prevents other people from seeing you when you're doing something you don't want anyone else to know about.

Tools and Ingredients

A piece of white paper

A pen or marker that writes black ink

A black pouch (preferably silk)

A piece of smoky quartz (cleansed)

A piece of jet (cleansed)

A piece of hematite (cleansed)

A pentagram

A crow's feather

Fern seeds (preferably gathered in the forest on Midsummer's Eve)

Clippings of your hair and fingernails

A black ribbon, 8" long

1. On the paper trace the outline of your left hand. Fold the paper three times and slip it into the pouch.

2. Add the gemstones, pentagram, feather, fern seeds, and clippings of your hair and fingernails.

3. Tie the black ribbon around the pouch to close it. Make eight knots in the ribbon, and each time you tie a knot, repeat this incantation:

"Whatever I do
Wherever I go.
No one will see.
No one will know."

4. Carry the pouch in your pocket whenever you want to be "invisible."

CUT THROUGH AN OBSTACLE TO LOVE

What's preventing you and a partner from enjoying a mutually fulfilling relationship? With this spell, you use the symbolism inherent in the witch's dagger, known as an athame, to cut through the obstacle. If the obstacle is another person, however, do not imagine injuring the person with your blade—a witch never uses an athame to do harm.

Tools and Ingredients

An athame (or dinner knife if you don't have an athame)

1. Bring to mind a problem or obstacle that is standing between you and your partner. In your mind's eye give this problem a form that you feel represents it vividly: a monster, a wall, whatever you choose. Imagine you are on one side of this obstacle and your partner is standing on the other side.

2. Hold your athame so that the blade points at the obstacle. Slash through the obstacle, moving your dagger back and forth until the obstacle is destroyed.

3. Now that your path is no longer blocked, envision moving toward your partner and embracing him or her. Say aloud: "This is done in harmony with Divine Will, our own true wills, and with good to all."

The Hindu God Ganesh

Ganesh, one of the most beloved of the Hindu deities, is depicted with an elephant's head. He's known for his ability to overcome obstacles.

SPELL TO STRENGTHEN A BOND WITH A PARTNER

Perform this spell with your partner if he or she agrees. Otherwise, psychically ask the other person for permission to cast the spell before you begin.

Tools and Ingredients

2 pieces of rope, one the same length as your height and one the same
    length as your partner's height

Salt water

Sandalwood incense

Matches or a lighter

1. Tie the ropes together in three places. Each time you tie a knot, visualize the bond between you and your partner growing stronger and more loving.
2. As you tie the knots, repeat an affirmation such as: "[Partner's name] and I pledge ourselves to each other in love, forsaking all others, now and always."
3. Sprinkle the knotted ropes with salt water, and then hold them in the smoke of burning incense to charge the spell.
4. Place the ropes under your bed.

Sweeten Your Spells with Incense

For thousands of years aromatic gums and resins have been used in sacred rituals. Scent triggers instantaneous reactions in the brain; inhaling certain smells can cause measurable responses involving memory, emotions, awareness, and more. That's one reason magickal workers include scents in their spells. The best incense is blended from pure gums, resins, and plant material without synthetic binders. You can even make your own by grinding up aromatic wood or resin (with a mortar and pestle or a coffee grinder) and adding finely powdered herbs or dried flowers.

SMOKE AND MIRRORS

Who were you in a past life? Did you know your current lover in another time and place? This spell awakens your inner sight and helps you travel back in time.

Tools and Ingredients

A black candle in a holder

Sandalwood incense in a holder

A mirror

Matches or a lighter

1. Set the candle and incense (in their holders) on your altar or another surface.

2. Position the mirror behind the candle and incense, and light them. The mirror should reflect the flame and smoke.

3. Turn off all other forms of illumination. As the candlelight flickers and the smoke swirls in front of the mirror, look at your reflection. Allow your gaze to soften. Say aloud:

> *"Shadow and light*
> *Expand my sight.*
> *Open a door*
> *To a time before*
> *And let me see*
> *A different me."*

4. Continue looking at your reflection for as long as you like while your mind drifts back in time. Notice changes in your expression, features, coloring, etc. Pay attention to impressions, emotions, and thoughts that arise. Don't censor yourself—strange ideas can be clues to a past personality.

5. When you've finished, extinguish the candle and write down your experiences in your grimoire. You may want to do some research into what you experienced to gain additional insight—you might be surprised at what you discover. If you feel comfortable doing so, share the experience with your partner.

Mercury Retrograde

The planet Mercury governs all forms of communication, written and spoken. Every four months the planet appears to shift its course and move backward in the sky for three weeks; astrologers refer to this as Mercury retrograde. When this happens, communication suffers. You may not think as clearly as usual and can have trouble expressing yourself adequately. Therefore, this is not generally a good time to do magick spells. Consult an ephemeris or online astrology site to determine when Mercury is retrograde.

"We come into this world with precious gifts that are meant to be shared, if each one of us takes the time to send healing and love into the world, we truly can change the lives of many and the world around us."

—JASMEINE MOONSONG

BLOOD, SWEAT, AND TEARS

What are you willing to shed blood, sweat, and tears for? Before you perform this spell think carefully about what you really want and what you'll do to get it.

Tools and Ingredients

A chalice or wineglass

Spring water, apple cider, or wine

A drop of blood

A drop of sweat

A tear

1. Fill a chalice (or wineglass) with water, cider, or wine.

2. Prick your finger and squeeze a single drop of blood into the chalice. Add a drop of sweat and one tear.

3. Stir the mixture with your finger three times—clockwise if you want to attract something, counterclockwise if you want to end or repel something—while you focus on what you desire. See yourself already attaining your wish.

4. With the liquid, dot the parts of your body that correspond to each of your seven major chakras, and then drink the rest of the beverage.

5. Say aloud,

"Blood, sweat, and tears I've spilled.
My greatest wish is now fulfilled.
As it's sought, so it's willed."

FUTURE PERFECT

This spell uses the magick of feng shui, the ancient Chinese art of placement, to help you create your ideal future. The colorful symbolism of the tarot adds positive vibrancy to this spell.

Tools and Ingredients

Matches or a lighter

A sage smudge wand or sage incense

The Nine of Cups tarot card from a deck you don't use for readings

3 objects that symbolize the future you desire

1. Stand at the door you use most often to enter or exit your home and face inside. The center section of your home farthest from you is known as the Future Gua.

2. Go to this spot, light a sage smudge wand or sage incense, and let the smoke waft into the air to clear away any unwanted, ambient energies.

3. Remove any objects that don't concur with your vision for your future.

4. Lay the tarot card face-up in a place where you can leave it for at least three days.

5. On the card, set the three objects you've chosen to represent the future you desire—a wedding ring, for instance, symbolizes marriage. Gaze at these items for a few minutes while you visualize the conditions they represent manifesting in your life.

6. Each day move these three objects around a bit to keep their energies activated while you focus on attracting what they symbolize. When you've finished, reposition them back on the tarot card.

7. As soon as a situation you've envisioned materializes, remove the respective object and replace it with something else. In this way you continue to consciously create your future.

TURN THE TABLES

Is your ex making life difficult for you? Or, is someone you don't like making unwanted advances? Turn the tables on that person with this spell.

Tools and Ingredients

A black candle

2 straight pins

A photo of the person who's
    annoying you

A candleholder

Matches or a lighter

A small mirror

1. The candle represents the person who's causing trouble—pin the photo on it. (If you can't obtain a photo, inscribe the person's name on the candle.)
2. Stick the other pin through the candlewick, and then place the candle in its holder and light it.
3. Set the candle on your altar or a table. Hold the mirror so that it reflects the flame and say aloud:

> *"Behold, this mirror is my shield.*
> *Your wicked ways will be revealed.*
> *Any evil that you do*
> *Will instantly turn back on you."*

4. Imagine the mirror deflecting harm away from you. When you've finished, extinguish the candle and remove the pins.
5. Melt the candle completely and bury the residue in a barren place far from your home.
6. Put the pins in something that belongs to your tormentor.
7. Hang the mirror on the outside of the door to your home, with the reflective side facing out, to repel unwanted energies.

SPELL TO PROMPT A DECISION

Are you tired of waiting for someone to act or make a decision? This spell encourages another person to show his or her hand and helps bring a matter to a favorable conclusion. You can also do this spell for yourself if you're having trouble making a decision and need a little push.

Tools and Ingredients

A bloodstone or carnelian (cleansed)

Gold nail polish

Ginger or cinnamon essential oil

1. Three days before the full moon, wash the stone, and then paint the Norse rune Teiwaz on one side (it looks like an upward-pointing arrow). On the other side paint the astrological glyph for the Part of Fortune (it looks like an X inside a circle).

2. Hold the stone carefully until the nail polish dries and while you envision a positive outcome.

3. Dot some essential oil on the stone. (Ginger and cinnamon are stimulating scents.) Say aloud: "This is done with good to all, harming none. Blessed be."

4. If you are friendly with the other person, give him or her the stone before the moon is full and explain your intention. If you aren't on good terms (let's say you're trying to get your estranged husband to sign divorce papers), put the stone in his or her home, car, workplace, or yard.

Chapter 12

WHAT'S THE NEXT STEP?

In the previous chapters you learned to use time-honored concepts and practices to enrich the love and happiness in your life. You formed a closer kinship with the earth and began viewing plants, stones, and the rest of nature's gifts in a special way. You came to appreciate lunar and solar cycles and how they affect life on earth. You established a more intimate connection with deities, spirits, and other entities that share the universe with you. Perhaps most importantly, you gained a greater understanding of yourself, your hopes and dreams, your talents and abilities, and your relationships with others. I hope that in the process you also enjoyed doing some of the spells and rituals offered in this book, and that you found them helpful.

So what's the next step? That depends on you. In my experience people who discover the magick in the world and in themselves rarely return to their old way of living. More often, they continue developing their magickal muscles, increasing their knowledge and using what they know to help themselves and others.

"Magic is believing in yourself, if you can do that you can make anything happen."

—JOHANN WOLFGANG VON GOETHE

EXPAND YOUR HORIZONS

Although this book focuses on love spells and rituals, you can apply the same ideas and techniques to do magick for other purposes—to attract wealth, advance your career, improve your health—just about anything you desire. My other books in the Modern Witchcraft series cover these areas and offer suggestions you may want to use. You'll also find a treasure trove of information about magick, witchcraft, and other occult subjects in books and online sites. Each author will have a unique perspective and set of experiences to share. I encourage you to delve deeper.

Learn about Different Schools of Thought

The material I've shared in this book is influenced by Wiccan ideology, although I've also included a bit about feng shui, shamanism, and kitchen witchery. As you continue your exploration into the world of magick, you may want to learn about ritual magick, chaos magick, alchemy, Santeria, the Kabbalah, tarot, astrology, runes, and so on. Most likely, you'll find some ideas appeal to you more than others. Rob's Magick Blog at robjo.wordpress.com covers a wide range of subjects to get you started. Everything you learn will help you grow as a magician.

Work with Other People

Some of the spells and rituals in this book are designed to be performed with a romantic partner. If you're in a relationship with someone who's open to doing magick with you, great! Spellworking together can strengthen your magick as well as your relationship. Perhaps you'll enjoy doing some of the sex magick spells in Chapter 10. You can learn more in my book *Sex Magic for Beginners*. I also found Donald Michael Kraig's *Modern Sex Magick* and Sirona Knight's *Love, Sex, and Magick* helpful when I first embarked on this path.

You might also consider spellworking with like-minded friends or a circle of other witches. Each person brings his or her knowledge, experience, and energy to the group. Everyone's contribution can benefit the development of the whole. Each witch is a torchbearer whose flame, when joined with the flame of others, lights up the world. If you can't locate any kindred spirits in your area, you may want to look online for people who share your interests. The Witches' Voice at www.witchvox.com is a good place to start.

CRAFT YOUR OWN SPELLS

As I've said earlier, in this book and others, personalizing spells can make them more powerful. That's because you invest more of your creativity into them and they hold greater meaning for you. Tap your unique talents. For example, if you're an actor you may enjoy choreographing dramatic rituals. If you're a gardener, botanical spells are a natural for you. If you're already adept at tarot, feng shui, or another esoteric subject, find ways to bring that knowledge into your spells.

> *"Magick happens when you step into who you truly are and embrace that which fulfills your soul."*
> —DACHA AVELIN, *EMBRACING YOUR INNER WITCH*

Experiment with Different Ingredients

For many spells you can mix and match ingredients to get the results you desire. If you can't find a particular item called for in a spell, you can usually substitute something else instead. For example, I often suggest using rose quartz in love spells because it's a beautiful stone, it's readily available, and it's inexpensive. You might prefer morganite, however, or pink carnelian or rhodochrosite. Each has a distinctive energy and one might suit your purposes better than another. Judy Hall's books are good resources, especially if you plan to do a lot of spells with crystals and gemstones.

As you saw in the previous chapters, you can use various tools for the same objective. To attract a lover you can do a candle spell, make a talisman, or concoct a potion. Try various tools and techniques to see which ones you feel most comfortable with and which ones produce the best results.

Work with Words and Images

Many of the spells in this book use affirmations or incantations. You can include words, phrases, chants, poems, invocations, songs, even entire stories in your spells if you like. Some people choose words from a language other than their native tongue because they have no mundane associations with Arabic, Sanskrit, or Chinese. The affirmations and incantations I've written for this book are suggestions only. I encourage you to compose your own.

The same holds true for images. Although many pictures and symbols mean similar things to most people, that may not be true for you. Some people associate black cats with bad luck, but witches often favor them as familiars. Experiment with a variety of images in your spellwork. The stronger your reaction to a particular image, the greater impact it will have in your spell.

Keep a Grimoire

A grimoire or book of shadows is a witch's journal of spells and rituals. This is where you write down what you did, how, when, where, with whom, and what transpired. Doing so enables you to see what worked well, what didn't, and what changes you might make in the future. A grimoire is your record of your journey along the magickal path and it chronicles your growth as a witch. To learn more, see my book *The Modern Witchcraft Grimoire.*

OTHER SUGGESTIONS

What other steps can you take to improve your ability and gain greater mastery of your craft? Each person you ask will probably give a different set of guidelines, some of which will be useful to you, some not so much. I offer these additional suggestions:

- Read a lot of books by different authors to gain a variety of insights and perspectives.
- Meditate regularly to improve your mental focus and your connection with your higher self.
- Set a schedule for yourself that makes magickal study and spellwork part of your everyday life.
- See the world as sacred, and acknowledge that you are part of everything else.
- Apply what you learn—study alone won't make you a witch.
- Start with simple rituals and spells, and then work up to more complicated ones.
- Don't get discouraged if something doesn't work out the way you'd planned; try to determine what went wrong and why, and learn from your mistakes.
- Practice, practice, practice—magick is like every other skill: the more you do it, the better you get.

As always, I encourage you to explore, experiment, and enjoy. Merry meet, merry part, and merry meet again. Blessed be.

INDEX

ABOUT THE AUTHOR

Skye Alexander is the award-winning author of more than thirty fiction and nonfiction books including *The Modern Guide to Witchcraft*, *The Modern Witchcraft Spell Book*, *The Modern Witchcraft Grimoire*, *The Modern Witchcraft Book of Tarot*, *The Everything® Wicca & Witchcraft Book*, *The Everything® Spells & Charms Book*, *Naughty Spells/Nice Spells*, *Good Spells for Bad Days*, and *The Everything® Tarot Book*. Her stories have been published in anthologies internationally and her work has been translated into more than a dozen languages. The Discovery Channel featured her doing a ritual at Stonehenge in the TV special *Secret Stonehenge*. She divides her time between Texas and Massachusetts. Visit her at SkyeAlexander.com.